BASIC SOCCER STRATEGY

By BRIAN LINDSAY DENYER

Basic Soccer Strategy

An Introduction for Young Players

Illustrated with diagrams
by John Lane

DOUBLEDAY & COMPANY, INC.
GARDEN CITY, NEW YORK

Library of Congress Cataloging in Publication Data

Denyer, Brian Lindsay.
  Basic soccer strategy.

  (Basic strategy books)
  SUMMARY: An introduction to the basics of both offensive and defensive
soccer strategy.
  1. Soccer—Juvenile literature. [1. Soccer] I. Title.
GV943.25.D46   796.33′42
ISBN 0-385-07977-X Trade
      0-385-07964-8 Prebound
Library of Congress Catalog Card Number 74–11816

Contents

Key to Diagrams

 **Direction of Ball**

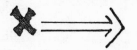 **Direction of Dribble**

 **Direction of Own Team Player**

Direction of Opposing Player

Preface

It is no secret that soccer is today the world's most popular sport, but many Americans are unaware of this extraordinary way of life. Unfortunately, there is little of the best soccer to be seen in the United States so that there remains much misunderstanding about the sport.

This book is, therefore, written to stimulate the curiosity of the young soccer player and to answer some of his questions. My intention is not just to explain to him *how* to play better, but rather to let him understand why soccer is played the way it is. I thereby hope the reader may enjoy his soccer more and thus *want* to play better. Tommy Docherty, Scotland's former National Team coach, once said that the lack of this enthusiasm and determination was the worst fault of all.

B.L.D.

PART I

Offensive Strategy

1

POSITIONS AND FORMATION

The two most important ideas in soccer are position and practice. By "position" I mean a player's not only being in the right position but *knowing* why he is there. If you do not know why you are in a certain position, then quite possibly you won't know what to do when you get the ball. By "practice" I mean the more physical aspects of the game—trapping the ball, passing, shooting, tackling, even conditioning and throw-ins. Unless you can play offensively *and* defensively, you are not an asset to your team. Playing soccer is similar to playing basketball and hockey where these ideas hold, but in soccer it is perhaps more difficult, since you are on a bigger field and have a larger number of team mates.

From the first two illustrations, you will be able to identify your position in two possible formations. All positions, except goalkeeper, belong to one of three "lines" or categories. These are 1) fullbacks, 2) halfbacks or links, 3) forwards. A formation will denote the number of players in each line. For example, the 3-3-4 formation will have 3 fullbacks, 3 halfbacks and 4 forwards. Remember, formations do not win or lose games; but they may help your team to control the ball more than the opposing team. Your coach will choose a formation to suit the individual players of your team. Depending upon the formation used, you may have to play a different position. Do not be upset. You must have qualities needed to play that new position or you would not have been chosen. Beside, a good soccer player can play any position if he has to—the result of an injury to a team mate, for example. Therefore, learn about all the positions on the field and understand what each player's responsibility is. After all, a fullback may find he has a chance to shoot, or a halfback may find himself playing center fullback.

Let's look now at the movement of your team when they are moving offensively.

These are possible movements only. Remember, you will have to move in relation to the ball. The player with the ball is not the most dangerous offensive person—the team mate who is unguarded and is in a position to receive a pass is potentially more dangerous. As a forward, do not hide behind an opposition fullback—

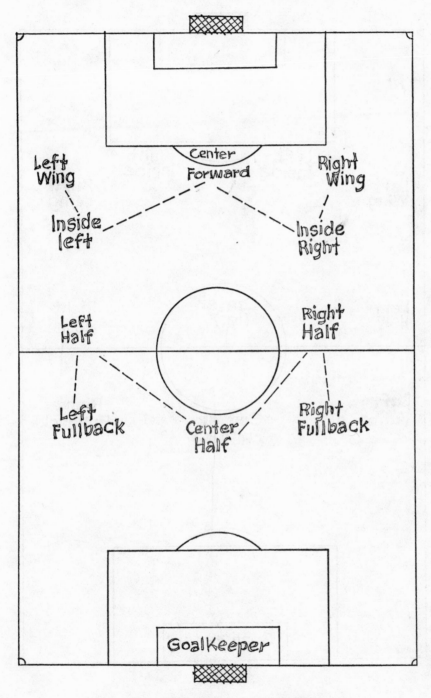

1. THE W-M OR 2-3-5 FORMATION.

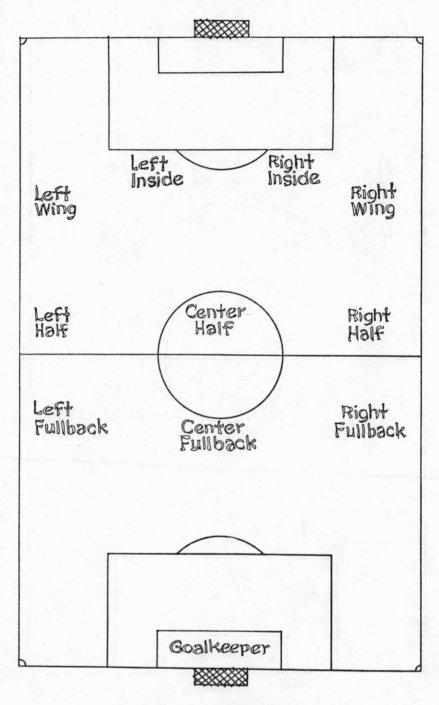

2. THE 3-3-4 FORMATION.

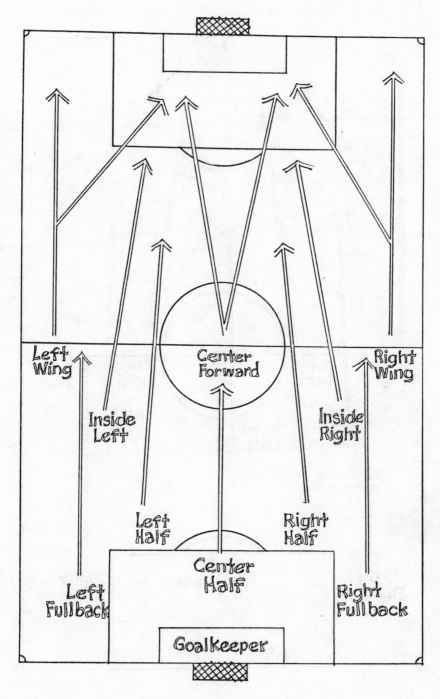

3. THE 2-3-5 ON OFFENSE.

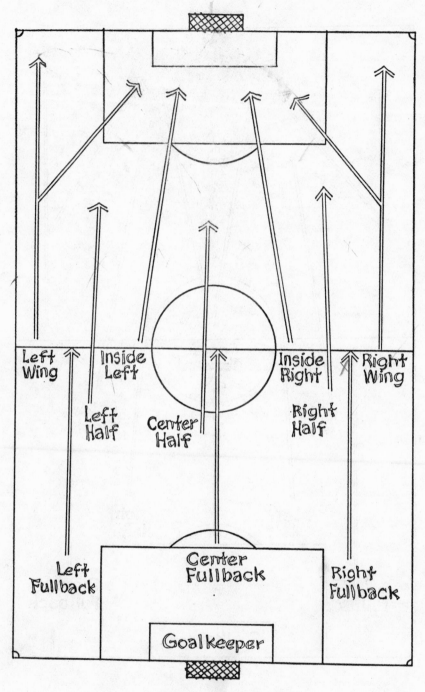

Left
Wing

Inside
Left

Inside
Right

Right
Wing

Left
Half

Center
Half

Right
Half

Left
Fullback

Center
Fullback

Right
Fullback

Goalkeeper

4. THE 3-3-4 ON OFFENSE.

even if you think you are in position. Move away from him into a position where the ball *could be passed* to you. Similarly, halfbacks, are you helping your team mate—can he pass to you? More specifically, once your team has control of the ball, the offensive responsibilities of players are:

For fullbacks: 1) To move quickly toward mid-field so that the opposition forwards must retreat with you, otherwise they will be offside. 2) To trail a halfback dribbling the ball in case he needs to pass back. 3) To cover the fastest opposition forwards so that they cannot outrun you for a fastbreak. 4) To pass the ball accurately rather than "boom" it downfield. You want to keep possession for your team. Many goals are scored from a movement that was started by a fullback's accurate ground pass.

For halfbacks: 1) To link the fullbacks and the forwards. 2) To control mid-field play with short, accurate passing that penetrates into the opposition half. 3) To move into an unmarked position and be able to receive a pass. 4) If you have the ball, to keep it moving. 5) To trail the forward who has possession of the ball. If you pass the ball to one of your forwards, back him up. 6) To be able to shoot effectively.

For forwards: 1) To be determined to score. 2) To be able to shoot with either foot. 3) To watch the offside and at the same time be ready for a long "through" pass. 4) For wings to be able to cross or chip the ball from the side of the field to the center of the field. 5) To move into a position to be able to receive a pass. 6) To stay on your own side of the field as an inside or wing. For example, the right wing should not be playing on the left side of the field. 7) To keep the space open in front of your team mate who has the ball. 8) Above all, to be able to penetrate, by passing or dribbling, deep into the opposing half of the field.

Other points for which all players are responsible are detailed later but, unless there is *movement without the ball,* offensive progress will be stopped except when the left half is an outstanding dribbler. Look at the diagram.

1. The center half should realize he is not open to receive a pass. His movement away from the ball creates an offensive threat if he is then passed the ball.

2. The right half moves laterally to receive a *square* pass. This moves the ball to the right side of the field and thereby causes the opposing defense to shift to its left.

3. The left fullback, as suggested, trails his halfback, moving upfield to use the open space and receive a *square* pass down the left side of the field.

4. The left wing "cuts back" so that he can receive a pass from the left half. A forward does not go just forward!

This may seem complicated, but a position in soccer is never a stationary matter. Moving without the ball is the key to offensive strategy.

Tips:

1. Know the positions and responsibilities of your team mates.

2. Move quickly out of defense toward the opposition's half of the field.

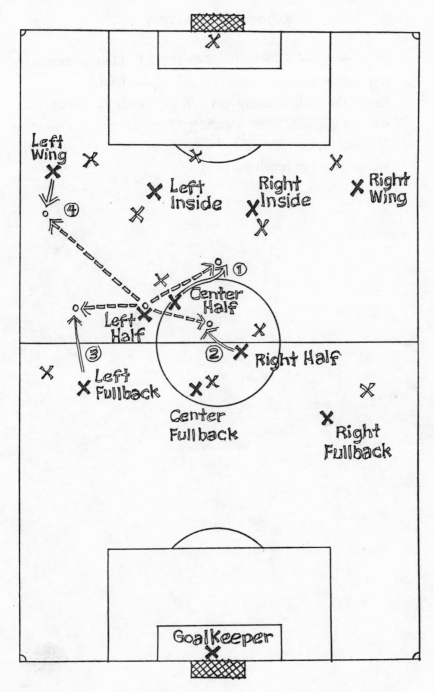

5. MOVING WITHOUT THE BALL TO BE ABLE TO RECEIVE
A PASS.

3. Stay on your own *side* of the field. (For example, left halfback stays on the left side of the field.)
4. Keep the ball moving on offense. Pass or shoot as soon as you see the opportunity.
5. If your team has the ball, move into a position where you can receive a pass.

2

KICKING

Kicking the ball into a goal is what soccer is all about. Beside shots at goal, kicks may be passes or fullback clearances. The variety of ways of kicking a soccer ball is what this chapter is about.

One of the most difficult points for a beginner in soccer to understand is that the toe kick is an inaccurate kick and is seldom used by a professional player. Every soccer player should learn to kick with 1) the inside of the foot, 2) the instep (the part of foot under the laces of the shoe), and 3) the outside of the foot. Moreover, he should try to develop these kicks with both feet. All other kicks are variations of these three basic ones. But in any kick, the key is keeping your eyes on the ball.

6. THE INSIDE-OF-THE-FOOT KICK.

1) The inside-of-the-foot kick:
Accuracy rather than power is the importance of this kick. A straight approach toward the ball is made. The non-kicking foot is placed some six inches away from the line of the ball. The kicking leg is turned outward so that the inside of the foot—from toe to heel—is facing the ball. Bend the knee so that the kicking foot clears the ground. Make a short back swing, brace the knee and foot for the kick, swing through, and push the ball. If the ball lifts off the ground, then your foot is too low. This kick is used for short accurate ground passing but can be used for longer passes with a flicking action.

2) The outside-of-the-foot kick:
This kick is used by any player sprinting downfield and just touching the ball with the outside of the foot. In this manner the ball will stay close and under control.

7. THE OUTSIDE-OF-THE-FOOT KICK.

At the same time, this kick hinders the player's stride less. Thus, it can also be used for a quick short pass and when the passer is running.

The kicker points the toes of his kicking foot inward. Swing back from the knee and flick at the ball. If you are dribbling at high speed, then you touch the ball just before your foot comes to the ground. The foot's momentum will carry the ball another five yards or more.

8. THE INSTEP KICK: "HEAD OVER THE BALL."

3) The instep kick:

This is your most powerful kick when done properly. The ball is kicked with the laces of the shoe with the weight of your body behind it. To kick low and hard at goal, for example, try not to break your stride in approaching the ball. Plant your non-kicking foot along-

9, 10.   THE INSTEP KICK.

side the ball and pointing in the direction of aim. As you do so, swing the kicking leg back from the hip with the knee bent and toes pointed down. Make sure your head is over the ball, otherwise the kick will not go low. Swing the kicking leg forward so that the knee comes over the ball. Keeping the toes pointed, straighten the knee at the moment of impact. Once you can do this kick fairly well, you can practice shifting your weight onto the kicking foot as you follow through.

A fullback clearing the ball, or a goalkeeper taking a goal kick, may want to kick the ball higher. The height in the kick depends upon how close the non-kicking foot is to the ball. For the clearance kick, or "lofted-in-step" kick, you should place the non-kicking foot about six inches back from alongside the ball. With practice, you should sense as you kick the ball how high the ball will rise.

Many young players stub their toes in this kick. The reason is *either* that they are straightening the knee too soon, *or* they are placing the non-kicking foot too far behind the ball.

4) The chip:
The chip kick is used to pass over the heads of your opponents: the wing may use this for crossing the ball. The halfback can use it to try to reach one of his forwards. It becomes effective to use against a team that does not head well, especially if your forwards can head properly.

The chip is kicked with the *inside* of the instep. It is not as powerful as the full instep kick, but then it is

11. THE CHIP.

easier for a team mate to control by heading it or trapping it. The chip is like a *hooked* instep kick, and you approach the ball at an angle so that your kick has to hook it. Again, the non-kicking foot is placed slightly behind the ball, but the back swing of the kicking foot will go outward, and you must point the toes *out* as well as down. Because of this outward swing the forward swing and kick will be with the *inside* of the instep—right above your big toe! This kick will need practice, but it will permit a wing to cross the ball when he is running straight parallel to the side line. Accuracy is difficult to develop, but the hardest thing about this kick is balancing your weight on the non-kicking foot.

5) The volley kick:

The volley kick is a first-time instep kick without trapping the ball. Often a fullback under pressure will have to use this kick. But, whenever possible trap the ball before kicking it so your kicks will be much more accurate.

Timing is the key with the volley kick. Try to have

12. THE VOLLEY KICK WITH THE INSTEP.

13. THE VOLLEY KICK WITH THE INSIDE OF THE FOOT.

your knee over the ball before your foot swings through with the kick. Again, eyes on the ball and the head almost over it as you kick.

6) The half-volley kick:

This is an instep kick on a bouncing ball. It is difficult to do well, but the half-volley kick is a powerful kick if timed right. Notice how the head and the kicking-leg's

14–16.   THE HALF VOLLEY.

knee are over the ball in the illustration, and notice the follow-through of this instep kick.

This kick can be used effectively by any player making a long pass, especially by a fullback under pressure. A forward could also use the half volley to shoot at goal; it will be a good, hard shot although not necessarily an accurate one.

Tips:

1. Keep your head down and eyes on the ball when kicking.

2. In all these kicks your knee should be over the ball at the moment of kicking.
3. Balance your weight on the non-kicking foot so that you follow through to make your kick accurate.
4. Develop these kicks with both feet.

3

PASSING

Soccer, like basketball and hockey, is a passing game. Even the world's best dribbler, Pelé, would agree with that. In a well-balanced game where both teams know their skills well, it is almost always the team that passes better who wins.

Once you and your team mates can kick fairly well, you will understand what I said in Chapter 1 about positioning: "If your team has the ball, move into a position where you can receive a pass." The receiver therefore creates the passing opportunity. If all players on a team are constantly thinking about making or receiving a pass, then they will become a good team. Moreover, it is better for each player to make a variety of passes, otherwise the opposing defense can easily anticipate a player's moves. Even a wing can occasionally cross low and hard instead of always chipping, as long as his team mates know about this possibility. Usually you should use the outside- or inside-of-the-foot kick for a short pass, and the instep kick for longer passes.

The square pass: This is so simple a pass that often a young player will forget to use it. It is quite valuable for use at mid-field. As the illustration shows, the square pass is a lateral pass from one side of the field to the center or opposite side. The reason for the left half's pass is that he is challenged and cannot find an unmarked man ahead of him to pass to; thus he passes "square" to cause the opposing defense to shift toward the center. With this shift, the other side of the field is now available for short passing too. Although the square pass does not penetrate offensively, there are more passsing chances created, and thus it often starts an offensive threat from mid-field.

The give-and-go (wall pass): The give-and-go is the

17. THE "GIVE-AND-GO" OR WALL PASS.

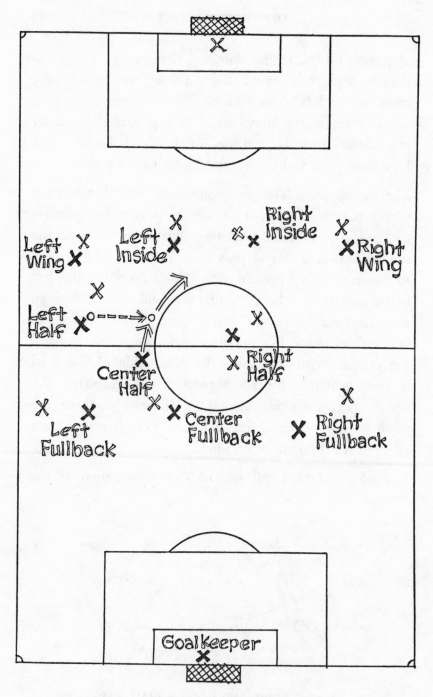

18. THE SQUARE PASS.

most dangerous offensive movement for a small space. The possibility of it occurs when you are faced with a two-on-two or two-on-one situation, and can be used at mid-field as well as inside the opponent's half. Often the ball carrier may be alone initially, but with a team mate cutting back to within seven or eight yards of him the ball can be passed and returned using the side of the foot kick. You, as the ball carrier, break behind your defender as soon as you have passed or given the ball to your team mate. The team mate must return a first-time pass since speed is essential. Moreover, it must be accurate, so both passes should be inside-of-the-foot kicks. Remember, you use the give-and-go only if there is space to receive that return pass.

19. BREAKING FROM A SHORT PASS.

If the return pass is anticipated by the defender, the receiver should himself break with the ball. He should then be looking for another quick pass, or even a shot on goal.

The through ball: As the name suggests, this pass goes straight through a defense. This is, of course, only pos-

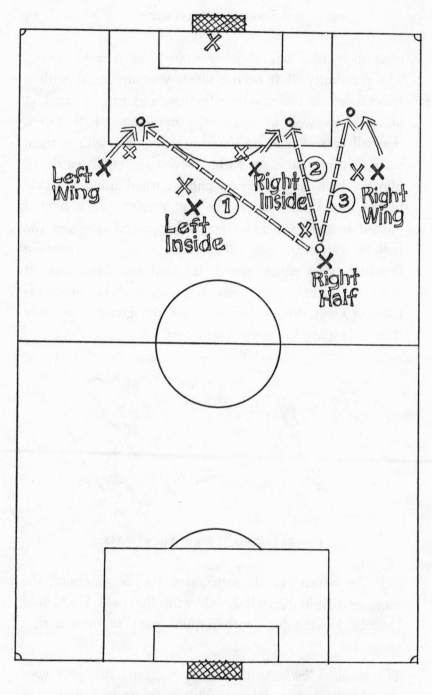

20. THE THROUGH BALL: THREE POSSIBILITIES.

sible if there is a gap in the defensive line or if the ball is passed in the air over the defenders' heads. Since it is a long pass, you will probably use the instep kick or the chip to clear the defenders' heads.

The illustration shows three possible through passes. In all three cases it should be noted that there is space for the team mate to receive the pass. By passing a through ball, you are using space that was "offside," thus penetrating the defense.

1) The first pass shows the right half chipping over the defenders to his left wing. Notice that the pass should be in front of the left wing in order to *lead* him toward goal. Often, however, this pass is not possible since the left wing's defender (probably the right back) may be already in that passing space and laying back in a "dog-leg" position.

2) This is the shortest through pass since it is kicked almost straight ahead. Thus, the inside-of-the-foot kick could be used. If you feel you cannot kick hard enough with this kick, use the instep kick. In either case, the right-half's pass must be on the ground so that the inside can play the ball immediately when he arrives at the ball. With a through ball down the center of the field, make sure the pass does not go to the goalkeeper, as a good goalie will be alert for this pass. On the other hand, this pass usually gives the inside who receives the ball a shot on goal.

3) The right half kicks a ground pass toward the corner flag leading his right wing to the ball. Use the instep kick for this pass and be certain there is a gap through which to pass the ball.

If the right wing is directly in front of the right half, the chip pass over the right wing himself and toward the corner flag could be used. In either case, the right wing will be in a good place to make a center pass.

The advantage of the through ball is not only penetrating the defense but also forcing the defender to run toward his own goal. It puts the offensive player on the advantage each time. However, there is the disadvantage of all long passes—the problem of accuracy. If the through ball is not kicked accurately, then your team will almost always lose possession of the ball—which means you cannot score!

The center (or cross): This pass is the high pass from the side of the field to the center, with the ball coming down within fifteen yards from the opponent's goal. It gives the offensive forwards an immediate chance to score if they can play the ball. Thus, there is often pressure and panic in the defense while scrambling for the ball in the air in front of goal.

It is most often the wing who has to center the ball, and he should do so with a chip kick. This ensures that the pass cannot be blocked or intercepted and that it must land in front of the opposing goal. The wing must practice the center pass so that he does not miskick the ball or give away a goal kick.

As the illustration shows, when a wing or offensive player is in the shaded area and has team mates in front of goal he should center the ball rather than shoot. If he is already inside the penalty area, pass accurately to the most open or unguarded team mate who will then have a shot. This may mean passing

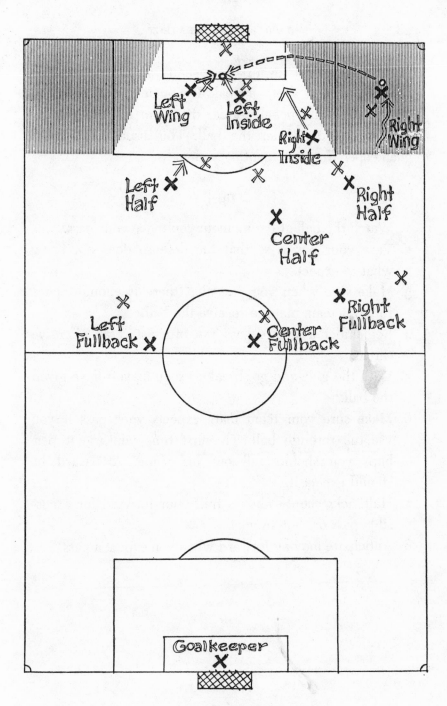

21. CROSSING THE BALL.

slightly backward toward the penalty spot, yet it should produce a good shot on goal. If you are in the shaded area outside the penalty area, then aim for the penalty spot when you center the ball. This usually stops the goalkeeper from intercepting your pass.

Tips:

1. Watch the ball at the moment you make your pass.
2. Vary your passes so that the defense does not know what to expect.
3. Make sure when you pass that there is enough space for your team mate to receive the ball.
4. Remember a square pass can often start an offensive threat.
5. With the give-and-go, break as soon as you have given the ball.
6. Make sure your team mate expects your pass if you use the through ball. The first time you use it perhaps you should call out his name. Afterward he should expect it.
7. Halfbacks should always trail your forward for a possible pass or shot on goal.
8. Anticipate moving forward when you expect a pass.

4

HEADING

Heading is an important part of soccer. A head ball can be a pass, a shot on goal, a clearance, or even a way of trapping the ball. Heading is the easiest way to play a ball in the air, and yet so many school players are afraid to head. There is little reason for this fear if your *forehead* is ready to meet the ball.

A good way to start heading is to practice with a team mate about your own size. Let him hold the ball with both hands, up in the air and just in front of you. Practice jumping to head the ball with the forehead so that the ball almost touches the hairline. At the moment of contact brace your neck so that the forehead hits the ball rather than the ball hitting the head. Keep your eyes open and watch the ball.

22. HEADING THE BALL WITH THE FRONT OF FOREHEAD.

23. HEADING THE BALL WITH THE SIDE OF FOREHEAD.

Once this seems easy start your jump facing sideways. Jump and turn to head the ball. You will use the side of the *forehead* (not the side of the *head*) to head the ball as you turn. You will use this way of heading when you are moving in one direction and heading in another. The neck should be cocked, or turned, in the opposite direction to where you are heading. The forehead then will hit the ball in the direction you want. In other words, to head to your left, cock your neck to the right and meet the ball with the left side of the forehead as it meets the ball. Practice using both sides of the forehead.

Now you can practice heading with a partner about five to ten yards away who throws a high ball to you. You may prefer not to jump to head at first. However, try to head accurately. Remember the forehead must meet the ball—not the other way round. Heading is a

24. "HEAD FROM THE WAIST UPWARD."

body action from the waist upward. The trunk of the body is cocked from the waist, then released to let the forehead "fire" at the ball. The neck is always braced as the forehead meets the ball. The snap from the waist is what allows players to head the ball over twenty yards.

When you are in a game, try to have both feet planted on the ground when you head, but if you are challenged by an opposing player jump to meet the ball.

The side of the forehead will need much practice to become an accurate head ball. Thus, the straight-on approach is easier, but you do not always have the chance to use it. Whenever you head in a game try to pass to a team mate, or at least away from the opposition. Heading on goal is another possibility for forwards, and will be discussed later.

Tips:

1. Always head with your forehead.
2. Always keep your eyes open and watch the ball onto your forehead.
3. Try to head from the waist to gain power in your head ball.
4. Always have your forehead meet the ball; not the other way round.

5

TRAPPING AND CONTROLLING THE BALL

Pelé was once asked what the most important thing in soccer was. He quickly replied, "Ball control." Even if you can pass and position yourself well, unless you can quickly control the ball when it comes to you, you are not a soccer player. The art of being able to immediately control the ball moving toward you is called *trapping*.

Various traps are discussed here so that a player can control a chest-high ball or low hard pass. In all cases you must once again watch the ball. Before trapping the ball you should have already looked around you to see what possible passes you might make. Moreover, all traps should stop the ball right in front of you. Five yards away is a poor trap and may well cost you possession of the ball.

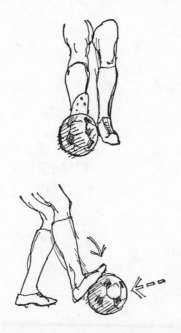

25–26. THE SOLE-OF-FOOT TRAP.

The sole-of-foot trap: For a ball coming along the ground, or about to bounce in front of you, this is the easiest trap. The trapping foot—you should be able to use either—is lifted with the toes slightly upward and held about nine inches off the ground. You wedge the ball between the sole of foot and the ground. The timing of this trap is all-important. As you wedge the ball you can gently move the trapping foot forward so the ball will be just in front of you, right where you need it to make a pass. The only disadvantage of this sure trap is that you have to stop your stride to wedge the ball, thus giving the opposition time to tackle you. One possible way out is to roll the ball away from an oncoming opponent with the sole of your foot as you trap the ball. After that, however, you had better move quickly.

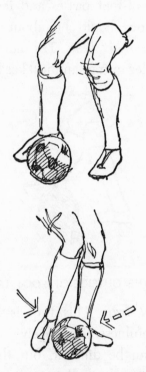

27–28. THE INSIDE-OF-FOOT TRAP.

The inside-of-foot trap: This can be a substitute for the sole-of-foot trap on a bouncing ball. Moreover, it can be used to control a square pass received from the side, or even to control a long low instep pass since you can change the height of your foot easily from thigh level to ground level.

Rather than wedge the ball, the inside-of-foot trap is better used when you are moving toward the ball. It is the reverse of the inside-of-foot kick. Extend the inside-of-foot to face the ball coming toward you. As you receive the ball, draw your foot back so that the ball does not rebound but stops right in front of you. Practice making inside-of-foot passes and inside-of-foot traps with a partner. You should be about ten yards apart, and practice with both feet. Try not to let the ball bounce as it is harder to trap and it takes longer.

29. THE OUTSIDE-OF-FOOT TRAP.

The outside-of-foot trap: This trap is less used, yet it does have its usefulness. To receive a pass that you have to run for can be difficult, but the outside-of-foot trap will let you stop the ball to control it in the direction you are running.

You turn the toes down as you trap it so that the outside-of-foot receives the ball—not the toe. With practice you should be able to use this trap for first-time control without breaking your running stride. For example, if you are running upfield to receive a square pass, you will be able to trap the ball with the outside of the foot and continue running upfield dribbling the ball.

30. THE THIGH TRAP.

The thigh trap: The thigh trap deals with a waist-high ball. Hold the knee up and turn it outward so that your thigh is parallel to the ground and facing the ball. At the moment of contact drop the thigh so that the ball will drop in front of you. To avoid any bouncing, you can immediately sole trap the ball. You do need time to use this trap.

The chest trap: Actually, a professional soccer player may use any part of the body—except the arms—to control the ball. However, the chest trap is the most common trap for a high ball, provided you have enough time to trap and pass the ball. If you do not have this time, perhaps you should head the ball.

Breathe in and stick out your chest to meet the ball,

31. THE CHEST TRAP.

with your arms braced back. At the moment the ball meets the chest, exhale so that your chest drops in and makes the ball drop down in front of you. Again, a quick sole-of-foot trap prevents the ball from bouncing around in front of you.

Tips:

1. Watch the ball right into your trap.
2. All traps depend on perfect timing: they need practicing.
3. Remember that you are absorbing the momentum of the ball.
4. If you do not have time to trap, try to use the inside-of-foot kick or head to pass to a nearby teammate.
5. Do not try to chip or kick long passes without first trapping the ball.

6

DRIBBLING

Unless you have a lot of space to run unguarded, pass rather than dribble. This point I cannot stress enough, since all players, once they have learned to control the ball well, love to dribble. If you dribble the ball, you can be certain that the whole opposing defense is shifting to cover your play. The longer you keep the ball, the closer you are guarded and the fewer become your passing possibilities. The illustration may seem to present an obvious choice—pass—but so many school players do not look to their sides at all.

If you dribble unguarded, then keep your head up and use the outside-of-foot kick to gently tap the ball ahead of you. Keep it close, otherwise you will not be able to stop when you want to. The wing is the most

32. "PASS TO THE OPEN PLAYER."

33. DRIBBLING WITH THE OUTSIDE OF THE FOOT.

frequent dribbler since he has more space to run in at the side of the field.

Dribbling around a defending player requires excellent ball control and much practice at one or two particular moves. As in basketball and hockey, these are

34–35. THE BODY FAKE OR FEINT.

your fake moves. Every soccer player should work on his own move to best suit his ability.

The body fake: The basic idea of a body fake is to lean one way to try to fake the defender into moving that way, then to break to the other side of him. You may even fake the kick by bringing your foot over the ball instead of kicking it. With the same foot you can then kick it the other way as you start to break. In fact, the body fake works best if it is combined with a kick fake. Remember to keep your balance so you can break quickly.

36–39. THE STOP-AND-GO FAKE OR FEINT.

The stop-and-go: The idea of the stop-and-go is to overcome the situation where you want to move into a space, but you are guarded by a defender. So you stop using the sole-of-foot trap, look up as if to make a pass in the opposite direction, then break with the ball in the direction you started. When you stop you can use a body fake if you want.

Whichever way you choose, dribbling around someone has to be done perfectly, and thus requires extra practice time. It should be noted, moreover, that forwards do most of the dribbling since you should pass and not try to dribble around an opponent when you

are in your own half of the field. There is generally
more space for dribbling on the side of the field rather
than the middle. It is, therefore, easier for a wing to
dribble around someone than for a center forward.

Tips:

1. Do not dribble if you can pass.
2. Do not dribble if you are in your own half.
3. Dribble with the ball in control at every stride.
4. Dribble with speed and with your head up. Look at
   the ball only to pass or to shoot.
5. All good fakes need practice.
6. Sprint when you break with the ball.

7

SHOOTING

Shooting is the most important offensive part of the game. If your team cannot shoot well, then your chances of scoring are small. In a game your team should be getting fifteen shots on goal or more. The shots that float over the goal cannot score, so do not count them!

Many school soccer players ask me when and from where to shoot. You look for a shot as soon as you come to the edge of or inside the penalty area. You shoot from there as soon as you have an unblocked shot on goal. If a fullback is between you and the goal, do not shoot. If you can gain a stride on him then you may have your chance to shoot. Also do not shoot when you are positioned on the end line even if you are in the penalty area. You have no angle on the goal, thus no chance of scoring. Instead, pass across in front of the goal where a team mate can have a good shot. When you shoot, try to keep the ball low. It is harder for a goal-keeper to save. The best shot is from the instep kick.

40–42. THE INSTEP DRIVE.

The instep drive: The first two points to remember about an instep drive are: 1) control of the ball—you cannot shoot low, hard, and accurate if you do not have control of the ball, and 2) keep eyes on the ball —do not look at the goal when you shoot. Once you have the ball under control and ready to shoot, choose which side of goal you want to aim for. Then use the instep kick to shoot. Make sure your non-kicking foot is beside the ball as you kick and that your head is over the ball. Make a good backswing before bringing the kicking foot onto the ball. Remember your knee comes over the ball before straightening the kicking leg, and the toes must be pointed down. Your instep should kick the middle of the ball. As you kick, let your weight change from the non-kicking foot to the kicking foot as you follow through with your shot.

As you develop your instep kick, you will add your own ideas to shooting on goal. Some players try to flick or snap the ankle as they kick as part of following through. I do not advise this until you can shoot well. However, all forwards should be able to instep kick with *either* foot; in fact, this should be a qualification to play on the forward line. For a halfback to be able to shoot with either foot is desirable but less imperative.

Although you may have seen many professional or college players shoot first-time (without trapping the ball) with both ground balls and air balls, you should not attempt it until you can shoot a controlled ball perfectly with either foot. The volley shot and especially the scissors kick look so impressive to watch, but they seldom produce goals. Beside the instep drive, you should practice a controlled half-volley shot and heading on goal. If you can master these three techniques, then you will be a dangerous forward for any defense.

43–45. THE CONTROLLED HALF-VOLLEY SHOT.

The controlled half volley: If the ball is coming to you off the ground, chest or waist high, then the best shot is to chest or thigh trap the ball. But instead of then using the sole-of-foot trap to stop the ball, instep kick the ball as it bounces. This is called a half volley. Again, lean over the ball and do not straighten the kicking leg until the knee is over the ball. Timing this kick may seem difficult at first, but it can give you a powerful shot on goal.

46. HEADING ON GOAL.

Heading on goal: Just as you try to kick low on goal, so too must you head down when you head on goal. To see or even to make a goal with a head ball off a chip pass is one of the beautiful attractions of soccer. If you have seen this done, you will remember the header jumping high so he can head the ball down.

Almost all heading on goal requires heading with the side of the forehead. If possible, keep your feet on the ground and move in anticipation of where the ball will come down. Have the ball come down in front of you rather than behind you since you will then still be able to play the ball. Watch the ball right onto the forehead and remember to head from the waist for power. Make sure your forehead is at least level with the ball when you head, otherwise you will head upward. This will make it easy for the goalkeeper to save, or you may even head the ball over the crossbar for a goal kick. Even though you want this "header" to be very accurate, you cannot let the ball deflect off the forehead. Rather you must strike the ball.

Tips:

1. You must have control of the ball to shoot.
2. Aim low, for it is harder for the goalkeeper to save.
3. Watch the ball, not the goal.
4. Put the weight of your body behind all shots.
5. Follow up your shots for rebounds off the goalkeeper or off the goalposts.
6. Early in a game test the goalkeeper by taking some long shots.

8

THROW-INS

Although a throw-in is not as valuable as a free kick, it should be used to penetrate offensively. Since there is no second whistle, the first person to the ball should quickly prepare to throw the ball in. As soon as you have a team mate ready to receive the ball, make the throw-in. Do not wait until the opposition has covered all your players. However, for the throw-in to be helpful, it has to be done correctly, otherwise the opposition can get the throw-in.

The rules state that the throw-in must be a two-handed throw from behind the head, with no spin on the ball. If you want a quick, short throw-in, stand with your feet together behind the side line and make

47. THE SHORT THROW-IN.

the throw-in. If you want more distance—for example, to lead your player down the side of the field—go back a few yards and use the "run-up" approach. You use the short run to gain momentum. As you take your last stride before you would cross the side line, stop in that stride and drag the toe of your back foot on the ground. Remember both feet must be touching the ground. As soon as you start that last stride, swing the ball behind the head with both hands. The forward motion of the throw has to start as your *front* foot touches the ground. Follow through with your arms, but keep the back foot down.

I have seen several soccer players, including some high school players, throw the ball over thirty yards this way, so start practicing. All players should be able to make a correct throw-in since you never know who will be closest to the ball when it goes out of bounds.

48.   THE LONG THROW-IN.

49.   LEADING THE PLAYER WITH A THROW-IN.

The illustration shows an easy "play" for a throw-in. Both your team mates come quite close to you—up to five yards away. If one of the opposing players covering your team mates fails to cover him closely, then you can throw-in to him. If both the opposition players are drawn toward you, then lead either of your players with a long throw-in over the defender's head. Make sure there is open space for the ball and your player. Note that in this play your team mates, by cutting back toward you, have *created* offensive space.

Tips:

1. Throw from the waist rather than from the shoulder only.
2. Try to snap the waist and the wrists when you throw long.
3. Remember to keep both feet touching the ground and behind the line—the line is in play.
4. Try to lead the team mate to whom you throw the ball, so that he can take the ball while moving.
5. Step into the field of play immediately after throwing in the ball to anticipate a possible pass back from the team mate you threw it to. Often you will find yourself unmarked in this situation.

9

FREE KICKS

You can never be certain as to how many free kicks your team may be awarded during a game, but whenever there is one it should be used effectively. Included in this chapter are corner kicks—which are, in fact, free kicks—and goal kicks—which are indirect. If you are unsure as to which fouls or violations result in direct and indirect kicks, then check the rules in Appendix I.

Corners: Whenever the defending team plays the ball over the end line beside their own goal, a corner kick is awarded to the offensive team. Although the kick must be taken from the corner of the field, it should result in a good scoring opportunity.

Unless the field is very wide, do not make a short

pass from the corner. Rather, use the time to make a long, high kick with the instep. The chip will not be a long enough kick for many players. Put your weight behind and *under* the ball as you kick. If you kick right-footed, then you will find the ball curving slightly to your left. Similarly, if you kick left-footed, then it will curve to your right. So make sure you do not give away a goal kick from an inaccurate corner.

If the opposition goalkeeper does not catch cleanly, then you should aim close to the goal—perhaps some five yards out. However, usually the goalkeeper can handle that corner kick easily, so aim for the penalty spot, which actually is twelve yards out. Many young goalkeepers prefer, in this case, to remain in their goal.

The illustration shows a possible setup for a corner on the right. The other forwards are positioned so they can run in at the ball. Notice the opposite side wing—in this case, the left wing—standing at the corner of the 6-yard box. This, I feel, is the best position for the far-side wing. He can easily pick up a loose ball coming through the area or move in to deflect a shot that is going wide of the goal.

The halfbacks position themselves to pick up a partial clearance. From this they should have a shot on goal if they are moving in as they receive the ball. However, be warned about going too far into the penalty area because you will leave a huge space behind you and the opposition could retaliate with a fast break.

Whenever the ball is deep in opposition territory, the fullbacks should move up to the halfway line. On a corner, the center fullback or defensive center halfback

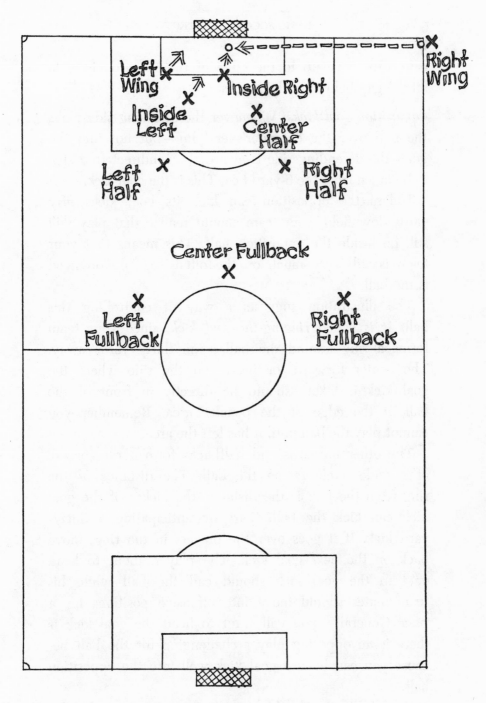

50. THE OFFENSIVE CORNER KICK.

can even move up to the edge of the 10-yard circle to fill the gap behind his halfbacks.

Opposition goal kicks: Whenever the attacking side plays the ball over the defender's end line—but not into the goal—the defending side is awarded an indirect free kick to be taken from the 6-yard box. This is the goal kick.

Unless the opposition can kick its goal kicks fifty yards downfield, your team should realize that play will still be inside the opposition half. This means that your team is still very much on the offensive. All you need is the ball.

The illustration suggests a way of controlling this ball. It is called *ringing-the-goal kick,* since your team forms a ring around the ball some thirty yards away. The center forward, or inside on the side where the goal kick is taken, should be directly in front of the ball at the edge of the penalty area. Remember you cannot play the ball until it has left the area.

The other forwards and halfbacks form a ring or arc of a wide circle facing the ball. The distance of the ring from the ball is the distance the kicker of the goal kick can kick the ball. Start by anticipating a thirty-yard kick. If it goes over the players in the ring, move back on the next goal kick. The player about to head or trap the goal kick should call the ball while his team mates should move into offensive positions for a pass. Generally, you will want to head the goal kick if there is an opposing player challenging for the ball because you can head a goal kick well into the opposition half.

Your fullbacks should not retreat too far on the op-

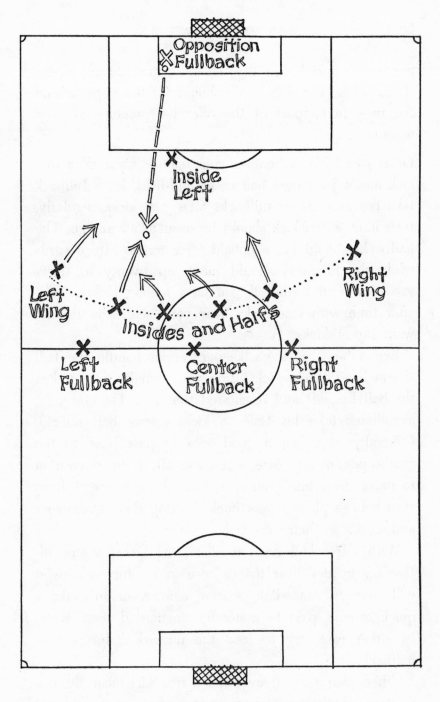

51. THE OPPOSITION GOAL KICK.

position goal kick, but they should anticipate any opposition break. Basically, they should fill the gaps behind the ring, in support of the offensive pressure of your team mates.

Other free kicks: Whenever your team is awarded a free kick inside your own half or at mid-field, let a fullback take the kick. Since fullbacks take goal kicks regularly, their long instep kick should be used to advantage. The halfbacks should move upfield some ten to fifteen yards while the forwards should move up twenty to thirty yards—or even farther if you have a long kicker. Take your time with free kicks near your goal; you do not want any miskicks.

Remember that a goalkeeper cannot handle the ball if you have a free kick inside your penalty area unless the ball has left and re-entered the area. Therefore, let a fullback take his time to kick a long ball upfield. Generally, it is not a good idea to pass back to the goalkeeper, in any case, since you allow the opposition to move deep into your own half. Even worse, I have seen college players pass back, beating their goalkeeper and scoring in their own goal.

With a free kick near mid-field, the kicker should either try to kick over the defense to his forwards, who will have an immediate scoring chance, or to make a quick ground pass to a nearby unguarded team mate. In either case, try to feed the unmarked forward or halfback.

When your team is awarded a free kick near the opposition penalty area, you want a shot on goal every

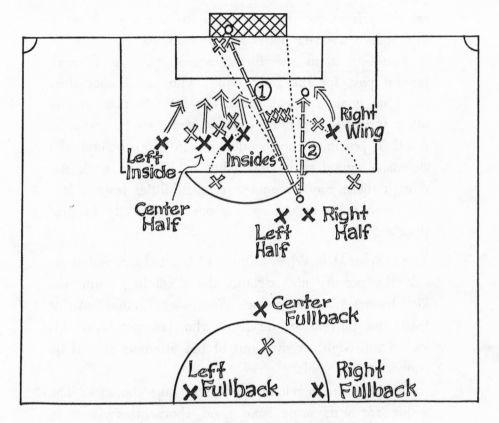

52. THE FREE KICK NEAR THE OPPOSITION GOAL.

time. If the free kick offers a good shot then you can expect the opposition to form a wall. If you have a player with a powerful shot, let him shoot directly, or tap the ball quickly to him in the case of an indirect free kick. This is possibility 1 in the illustration. The other forwards should follow up the shot anticipating a rebound. Watch offside! The halfbacks should hold their positions to pick up a clearance kick or header from the opposition, with the center fullback filling the space behind the halfback. Whoever takes the kick can ask the referee for the opposition to be ten yards away so that he can have a better shot on goal.

Possibility 2 in the illustration suggests a through ground pass for the right wing, who can immediately shoot on goal. You can make the through pass to any other forward, depending on the gap that is available. Another possible play would be to chip behind the defensive line for the left wing to head on goal. Although there may be numerous possibilities from a free kick, you want to choose the one most likely to produce a goal.

The penalty kick: When a direct kick is to be awarded inside the penalty area against the defending team, the kick becomes a penalty kick. Your team should have at least one player on the field who has practiced this kick a lot. Eight or nine out of ten attempts should be converted into goals.

Generally, an inside forward will take the kick. The inside forwards must have good shots—otherwise they should not be playing forward—so let an experienced shooter take the kick. Since the goalkeeper cannot move his feet until the kick is taken, he does not have much chance of saving a penalty kick. The kicker should not fake the kick, but should shoot accurately low and hard —and in that order of preference. Decide to which corner you are kicking as you place the ball on the penalty spot. Try not to look at the chosen corner when you are about to run up to the ball—it will tell the goalkeeper which way to dive. Rather, look at the ball with confidence, knowing where you are to put it. Do not look up until you have seen your foot kick the ball. Generally, the best kick is the instep kick to make sure it is low. However, it is then easy for the goalkeeper to see which way you are aiming. Practice with the inside of the foot can produce the low and accurate kick, but it is not very powerful. Each penalty kicker must then decide what gives him his best chance of scoring. One last point, always wait for the referee's *second* whistle before taking the kick. Just stare at the ball while you wait for that whistle. Keep your head!

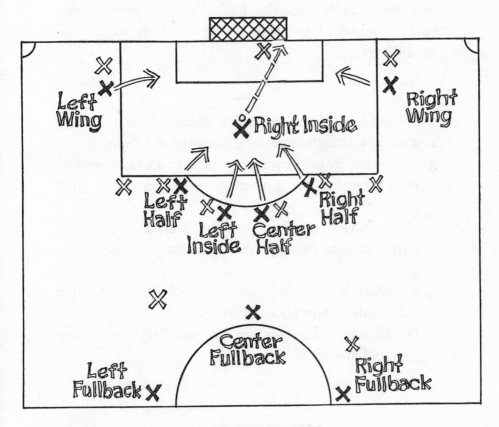

53. THE PENALTY KICK.

In the illustration of a penalty-kick situation, notice the position of the wings on the outside of the penalty area and the other forwards and halfbacks around the penalty arc. Remember, no one can be inside the arc on the penalty kick. All these players should be ready to follow the shot on goal for a possible rebound. Keep outside the area until the kick has been taken—do not enter when the second whistle goes. As soon as the kick is taken you should sprint a few yards toward the goal anticipating the rebound. Should the goalkeeper save the penalty kick the halfbacks will have to run back to mid-field to cover a fast break in support of the fullbacks.

Tips:

1. All free kicks should be used to threaten offensively.
2. Free-kick situations must be practiced as a team.
3. If you are to take corners or penalty kicks, you need extra practice. To give away goal kicks is a great waste.
4. If you have a set play for a free kick, have an alternative in case the opposition prevent you from doing it.
5. Concentrate on your *own* responsibilities; let other team mates worry about theirs.
6. On all free kicks there are two whistles; one to stop play and another to restart.

PART II

Defensive Strategy

10

DEFENSIVE
COVERING

As in basketball and hockey, in soccer you cannot play defense unless you have *position* on your man. This simply means positioning yourself between the opposing player you are guarding and your own goal. In this way, if your man has or is about to receive the ball, you will be able to prevent his progress toward your goal.

This understanding of guarding or *covering* a man is for all members of the team. It is everyone's responsibility to play defense when your team has lost possession of the ball. The first and most important defensive move is for the team mate nearest the ball to run after the opposing player to try to steal the ball back. Everyone else on your team, including the forwards, should *run* backward at least five yards, when they must look for an opposition player to guard. The basic direction to move for defensive positions is shown in the illustrations.

Although it may not seem clear just whom you should cover, the best idea is to look toward your own goal. Is there a man unguarded and no one moving to cover him? If so, you should pick him up. Consider your own area first. For example, the left half should worry about the left side of the field. As a rule, it is best to cover the opposing player nearest you.

The next illustration shows the opposition right halfback intercepting the ball. Your left inside should try to steal back the ball as other team mates move quickly to cover a man each, including the other forwards. Generally, the left and right fullbacks will cover the opposition wings as the center fullback and halfbacks cover the opposition in the center of the field.

Defense calls for complete understanding among team mates. Talk to each other, tell your team mate next to you whom you are covering. The center fullback in the illustration should tell the center half to cover the opposition right inside as he himself moves to cover the opposition left inside. You won't know their names or even their correct positions. Merely point to the opposition player and call to a team mate, "I've got him." Without talking, opposition players are left unguarded to penetrate your whole defense and possibly score or set up a scoring opportunity.

At mid-field on defense, the situation developing could be similar to the illustration, where the opposi-

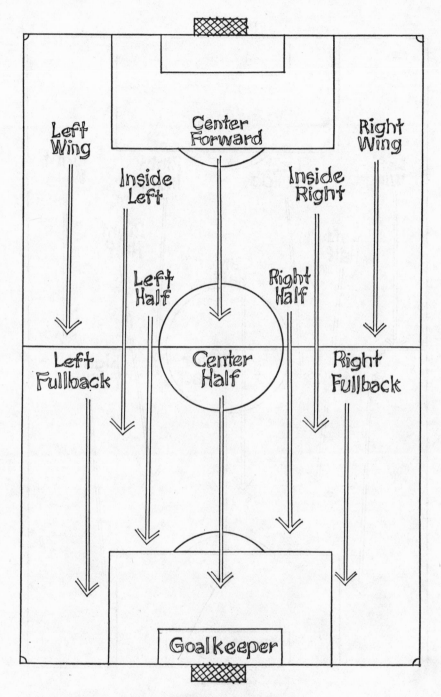

54. THE 2-3-5 ON DEFENSE.

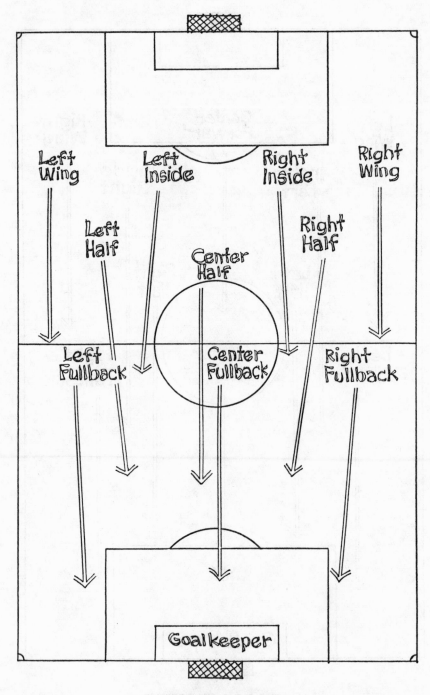

55. THE 3-3-4 ON DEFENSE.

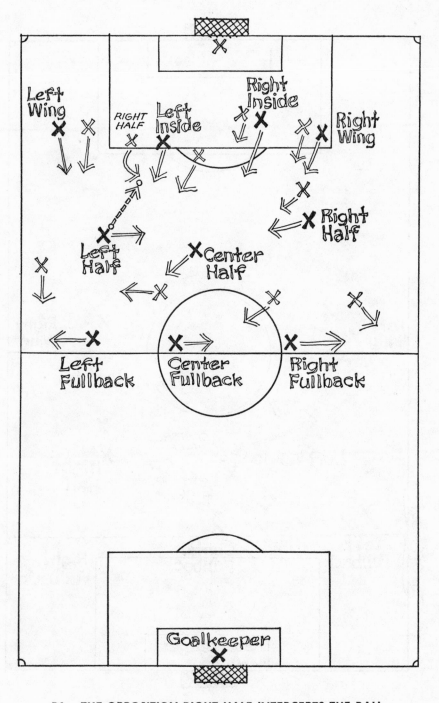

56. THE OPPOSITION RIGHT HALF INTERCEPTS THE BALL.

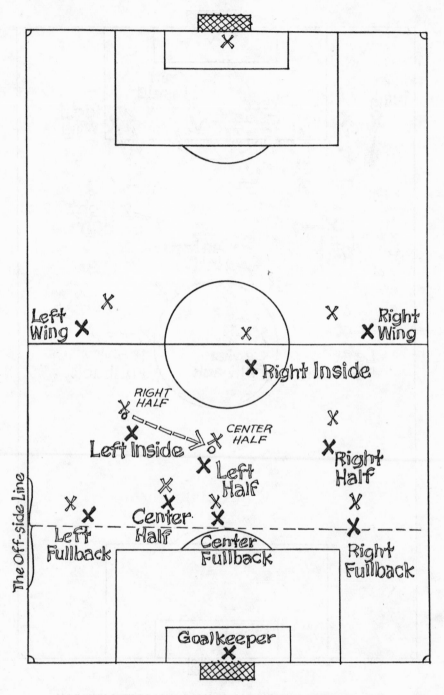

The Off-side Line

Left Wing

Right Wing

Right Inside

RIGHT HALF

Left Inside

CENTER HALF

Right Half

Left Half

Center Half

Left Fullback

Center Fullback

Right Fullback

Goalkeeper

57. SETTING UP THE DEFENSE WITH AN OFFSIDE LINE.

tion is seeking to penetrate your defense. In this particular case, the fullbacks are holding an *offside* line. The
advantage of this is to stop the opposition forwards
from moving too near your goal. If they go nearer your
goal, then they "no longer have two men between
themselves and their opposition goal." In other words
they will be offside if they are passed the ball. By keeping this lateral line, you limit the space the opposition
has for passing. Moreover, if it is used, the fullbacks
must remind each other about holding the offside line,
and they must also tell their own halfbacks not to cover
behind this line. If the halfback holds the line, then
the opposition player will have to stop, too.

The disadvantage of the offside line is that the
through ball can use the space behind the fullbacks. As
soon as the through ball has been kicked, it is an open
race between the fullbacks and the opposition forwards
for the ball. Therefore, if your team has slow fullbacks,
it is better not to hold an offside line but simply cover
the opposition forwards wherever they go.

A good passing possibility is shown in the illustration
where the opposition center halfback's pass to his left
wing penetrates your defense. The right fullback should,
in fact, be ready for this. However, if the pass lets the
opposition wing inside him to receive the pass, the center fullback should cover the left wing. On defense you
should always be thinking of helping your team mate,
of backing him up in case of mistakes. Notice, too, how
your center halfback should then move to cover the center fullback's man, and how the left fullback also moves
toward the middle to cover.

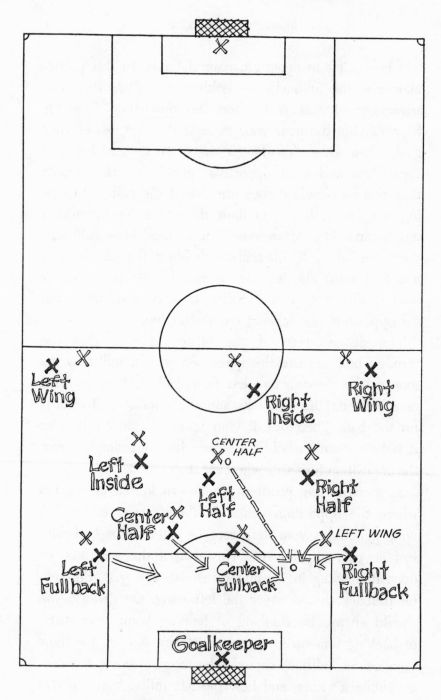

58. COVERING AN OPPOSITION THROUGH BALL.

The illustrations and situations discussed in this chapter have presented only a few possibilities for defensive covering. Another popular way is the *dog-leg,* shown in following illustration. This defense allows the left fullback on the side of the ball to limit the passing space on his side, while the center halfback is able to support him from behind. The end of the *leg* is the right fullback who has retreated quite close to his own penalty area. From this position he can cover not only the opposition left wing but also their forwards in the center of the field, supporting his center fullback. The dog-leg, then, gives depth in defense although it can allow the opposition to move deep into your own half of the field.

Whatever ideas your fullbacks have about defense, they have to be understood by all defenders, even substitutes. Remember to talk to each other so that no matter what the opposition does, your defense will have every opposing player covered. Once each of them is covered, your major duty is to stay between that player and your goal. In this way their shots on goal will not be open ones; rather they will be desperate ones which, hopefully, your goalkeeper can save.

The goalkeeper is his own man. The penalty area is his territory, and when you are in your own penalty area you must listen to him. The fullbacks direct the defense outside of this area, but inside of it your goalie is your leader.

Tips:

1. Try to recover the ball after losing possession.
2. Move quickly into a defensive position, and cover an opposition player.

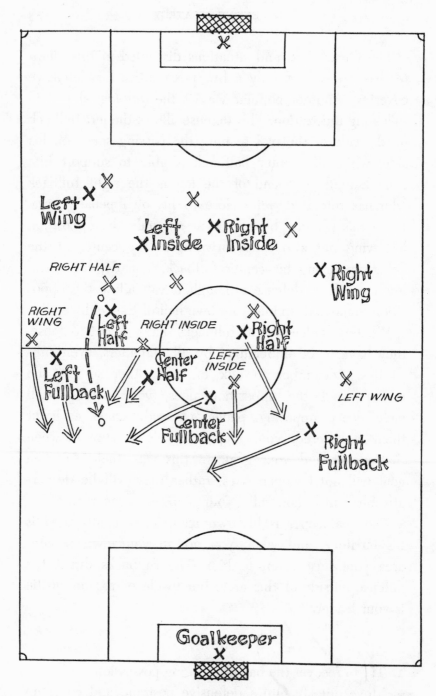

59. DEFENSIVE COVERING WITH A DOG-LEG.

3. Talk to each other as to who is covering an unguarded opposition player.
4. Always be ready to switch men if a team mate loses or is beaten by his man.
5. Inside your own penalty area, listen to your goalkeeper's instructions.

11

TACKLING AND RECOVERY

Now that you have an idea of your position on defense, you may be faced with the situation where the opposition player you are covering receives the ball. If possible, you should challenge for the ball so that he does not receive it, or at least tackle him before he gains full control of the ball. By tackle, I mean taking the ball away from the opposition with your feet. Remember, tackling in soccer does not permit you to use any part of your body on the opposition player, except the shoulder when you are trying to play the ball. Above all, your tackling foot must kick the ball, not the opponent. A trip will cost your team a direct free kick.

The most important point about tackling is timing. You want to tackle the opposition player with the ball when he does not have full control of the ball; that is, either when the ball is still in the air or when it is more than one pace from him. Never try to tackle a player front-on when he is standing with the ball stopped at his feet. He can easily go around you as you come toward him. Rather, let the ballplayer decide in which direction he is to move. As he moves with the ball, look for a moment when he does not have full control. This is your chance to try to steal the ball. You must

60. TRYING TO INTERCEPT THE BALL.

watch the ball, not the player's feet, otherwise he will use
a fake and go around you as you move the wrong way.

61.   THE BLOCK TACKLE.

The block tackle: This is the most effective tackle because when you tackle this way you can use the weight
of your body and your shoulder to help win the ball.
Whenever you decide to make the tackle you must
make it with determination and confidence. If you lack
confidence, you may hesitate and so lose your chance
to tackle. If you lack determination, you will not put
the weight of your body into the tackling foot. Then
you will not only lose the ball but possibly get hurt.
When two people collide it is almost always the person
who has less momentum (weight and speed) who gets
injured. This applies especially to tackles where the collision is on the ball. The tackler uses the inside of the
foot to make the tackle and leans with his shoulder
over the ball. Make sure you use your weight to follow

through so that the ball is forced forward in your direction.

62. THE SLIDE TACKLE.

The slide tackle: The slide tackle is similar to sliding in baseball. However, instead of a base, you are reaching for a moving ball about to be kicked by an opposition player. The purpose of the slide tackle is to push the ball away from a player with the ball who has *position* on you. In other words, you are no longer between him and your goal. As a desperate effort to stop him from running past you or from shooting on goal, you make a running slide at the ball. As you reach for the ball with one foot, tuck the other foot underneath you to break your fall. The kicking foot will toe the ball away—or, if you can, instep-kick it by turning your foot.

This tackle needs much practice for if you miss the ball you can easily trip your opponent or he can run past you, helpless on the ground. If you still have position on him, but only just, it is safer to try to run onto the ball and kick it out of his path. Beside kicking the ball out of reach of one opposition player, you should also try to kick the ball out of bounds to prevent another opposition player from continuing his offensive threat.

63. SWITCHING MEN AFTER MISSING A TACKLE.

In either tackling situation, should you be beaten, then a team mate must cover the opposition player with the ball while you must recover immediately to cover the man now left unguarded. This is called switching men, and you should call "Switch" as you would in basketball. It is a simple swap of covering responsibilities between two team mates, and no one else on the team should leave his man open as a result of the switch.

Although all players should be able to make the block and the slide tackle, the fullbacks have to practice until they believe they cannot be beaten on a tackle. A fullback will have more time to cover an opposing forward, and so he should always position himself with the attacker on the side he wants to tackle. Generally, that would be your right side. However, a fullback or halfback covering an opposition wing should position himself slightly to the outside of a wing with the ball. You will then prevent this wing from his instinctive move, which is to dribble down the side line. This will irritate a wing and force him into poorer moves. In covering a wing with the ball, you should give him more room, say five yards, instead of two, since wings are usually good sprinters. This positioning and moving to restrict an attacking player's movement is called *jockeying*.

Clearing: Whenever you win possession of the ball in your own third of the field, it is important to remember two things. The first is not to stand still with the ball, keep running as you look to make a pass. The second is not to run or pass toward the center of your own third of the field, since that is where the opposition attack men want the ball to be. A good clearing pass is shown in the illustration where the center fullback passes to the *outside*, finding his left half unmarked. Good trapping and a quick pass to the outside can often lead to a fast break or counterattack.

Tips:

1. Practice timing your tackles, especially in wet weather.
2. Use your weight and shoulders in the block tackle.
3. Practice kicking with the instep in the slide tackle.
4. Do not rush in to tackle; let your man come toward you.
5. Jockey the ballplayer to the side you want to tackle.
6. Call "Switch" if you miss a tackle.
7. Clear to the outside from your own third of the field.

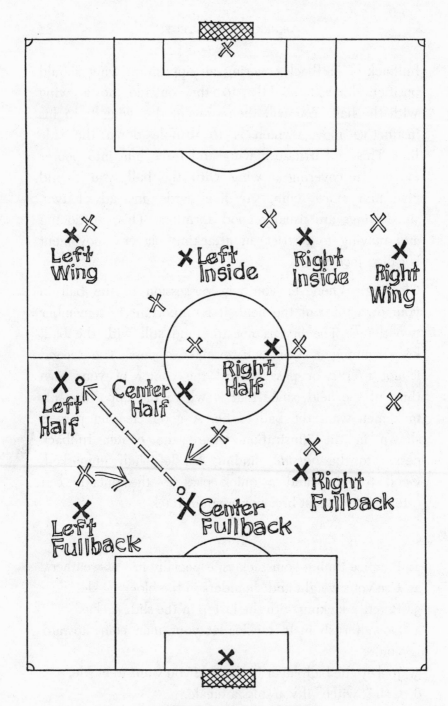

64. CLEARING TO THE OUTSIDE.

12

GOALKEEPING

Since the goalkeeper is the only player on the team who can use his hands, he must be able to use them to full advantage. He should be able to catch a high ball above his head before an eager forward has a chance to head the ball. He must be able to hold on to a hard shot and not let it rebound off his chest. He must be able to catch and hold a ball while in mid-air diving. He must be able to slide at a threatening forward's feet and snatch the ball away. In any of these goalkeeping actions, if he fails to hold onto the ball, he may have given up a goal. If a goalkeeper does not believe he can catch the ball without error, then he should not be playing in that position. His is the most responsible position on the team, and he must *want* this responsibility.

There are four rules that you, as goalkeeper, must never forget. The first rule says that you must move *instinctively* behind the line of the ball. If the shot is harder than you think it is, or if the shot dips so that the ball slips through your hands, your body or your legs will stop the ball.

The second rule is to watch the ball right into your hands when you catch it. Do not look at an opposing forward rushing in at you. You will learn to expect him, and you cannot afford to fumble that ball.

Rule number three is to recover immediately if you should make a mistake. I have seen many goalies stand and sulk because they have made a mistake. You do not have time to think about your mistake, you must think about where the ball is if it is no longer in your hands. I remember seeing a goalie dive for a rising shot. He missed the ball but it hit the crossbar and rebounded toward the penalty shot. The player who had shot the ball trapped the ball and shot it again. Somehow the goalie had recovered his position and was able to dive for this second shot—and saved it. It was a brilliant save thanks to his instinctive recovery of position.

The last rule is to know at all times where your goal line and your goalposts are. You will see a hockey goalie hit his goalposts with his stick without looking behind him to see where the posts are. His eyes are on the puck. In soccer a goalie must learn to watch the ball and still know where his goalposts are. Fortunately, in soccer you may have enough time as play comes toward you to look quickly at your goalposts. You must know, too, where the goal line is. I have seen many goals scored because the ball went over the goalie's head and beyond his reach. The goalie did not know where his crossbar and goal line were. The crossbar is eight feet high, so it is a good idea to wait one yard out from your goal line until you know where the ball is coming down. If you stay on your line or one yard out from it, then you can always go forward to catch a shot or a cross. However, you will soon learn how difficult it is to catch a ball over your head while moving backwards. If you suspect that a high shot is to come down near the crossbar, step onto the goal line and wait until you catch the ball. You may have to jump straight up to reach the ball, but unless you are under five feet tall you have no excuse for not catching a high shot on your goal line. There are times when you will have to leave your goal line and even times when you will have to tip the ball over the bar. These occasions are discussed later in this chapter.

Catching a low ball: If the ball you are to save is chest high or lower, first position yourself in line with the path of the ball. If it is moving slowly toward you, go to meet the ball, otherwise an opponent may beat you to it. You should avoid letting a ball bounce in front of you as you prepare to catch it for it may not bounce where you expect it to—especially if there is spin on the ball or if the weather is wet. Catch the ball with your palms facing the ball and your thumbs outward. Above all, whether you catch the ball at your feet or at your waist, gather the ball into your chest. In this way, should anyone nudge you, you will not lose the ball. Try to stand with your feet together, rather

than kneel, behind a ball on the ground so that you
can recover quickly if you make an error.

65.   "ALWAYS GATHER THE BALL INTO YOUR CHEST."

Catching a high ball: If it is a high ball, that is head
high or even higher, always jump to meet the ball. You
will have to practice your timing for this jump. It is always easier to catch a high ball that is level with your
head when you jump than to catch it with your arms
outstretched above you when you are standing.

To catch the high ball, have your arms outstretched
in front of you, with the palms of your hands facing
the ball and with your thumbs pointing toward each
other. Your thumbs may even be touching for you want
to make sure you have enough of each hand behind
the ball to stop it. Make sure you watch the ball right
into your hands. Once you have caught it, bring the
ball down to your chest to protect it. If you hold the
ball up there, an opposing forward may head the ball

66. CATCHING A HIGH BALL.

out of your hands just after you have caught it. Most goalies will jump off one foot—some will use more of a running start than others—but almost always the experienced goalkeeper will raise the other foot so that your knee can protect you from charging opponents. Remember, on a high cross—especially from corner kicks—to watch for the inswinger or outswinger. Learn to anticipate the curve of a high ball.

Punching the ball: Punching the ball instead of catching a high shot or cross should be used only when an opponent is jumping up with you so that his head interferes with your catching the ball. When you punch, use two hands if possible and straighten your arms as you punch the ball. It is often easiest to punch the ball back in the direction it came. If you try to direct it elsewhere, you may miss the ball altogether.

67. PUNCHING A HIGH BALL WHEN CHALLENGED.

Tipping the ball over the bar: As with punching the ball, this is done only when the high shot is too hard to catch or is about to hit the crossbar. In either case, the goalie should be close to his line so he will know whether the shot is to come down on the goal.

To tip the ball over the crossbar, jump up on your goal line with your stretched arms and your palms facing forward and upward. The ball, on hitting the palm, will be deflected up and over the bar. Do not, however, try to slap the ball, or it may drop into the goal behind your head. You are trying to deflect the ball upward, not to stop it.

68. A DIVING SAVE.

Diving: Sometimes the only possible way to stop a shot is to dive for the ball. Whenever you dive, push off with your feet so that you reach the ball quickly. Dive on your side so that your body lands behind the ball's path. Again watch the ball carefully and try to catch it. If you do, come down on top of the ball to smother it. However, if you know you cannot catch it, then try to push the ball toward the side line. You should not slap the ball down in front of your goal but rather try to push it to the side of your goal. Then if you have time, regain your feet and recover the ball. Often the ball will go out for a corner, but this is much safer than letting the ball bounce around in front of your goal with you on the ground.

One-on-one: One of the most frequent times a goalkeeper has to dive is when an opponent has beaten the last fullback and it is one-on-one—yourself and the player with the ball. Generally, you will want to meet him about ten yards out. A college goalie will be able to drive out fifteen yards, but do not become too reckless. As soon as the opponent has beaten your last team mate, move toward him with your hands out in front of you ready to save the ball. If he is in front of your goal, go to meet him as soon as he enters the penalty area; that is, eighteen yards away. If he is coming from the side of your goal, wait until he is about twelve yards away. When you leave your line, do not change your mind; run out and slide your feet out from under

69. COMING OUT ON A BREAKAWAY.

you to dive at the ball. You should go down whenever he is about to shoot, or if you do not give him that opportunity, when you are about five yards away from him. Your waist should come down in line with the ball.

Extend your lower arm close to the ground to block the ground shot, and use your other hand to block the higher shot. Kick your legs out to block the shot toward the other side of your goal.

Remember, if the opponent loses control or does not shoot, snatch the ball and gather it into the chest. Once you decide to go out and dive, do it—do not hesitate. You will not get hurt because if the opponent kicks you, he will be sent off the field. Moreover, a save like this can inspire your team since it frustrates the opposition.

Angles: Angles are the most important part of goal-keeping tactics. This term refers to the angle the player makes with your goalposts. Simply stated, you want to

70. THE WRONG ANGLE.

be in the middle of that shooting angle. In the illustration of the wrong angle, the goalie has neither moved far enough out toward the shooter, nor has he positioned himself in the middle of the shooter's angle. However, in the illustration of the right angle, the goalie is in a position to be able to reach any shot made. The goalkeeper's movement in this illustration is called *narrowing-the-angle.* Obviously, the closer you are to the shooter, the less area of the goal he has to shoot at. However, the closer you are to the shooter, the less

71.   THE RIGHT ANGLE.

time you give yourself to react to save his shot. The farther out you can dive and save, the less distance you have to approach the shooter. Narrowing-the-angle is a valuable skill all goalkeepers must develop because if you are not in the correct position, you will be unable to make the save.

Clearing the ball: The goalkeeper, once he has saved the ball, can choose either to punt the ball downfield or to throw the ball to a team mate. The punt generally gives you distance in clearing the ball but not necessarily accuracy. The throw is much more accurate.

A general rule for deciding which clearance to make is to look for your wings or halfbacks at the side of the field. If you see a team mate open in this position, try to throw the ball to him quickly. Do not bounce the ball for during the time that takes, your open team mate may be covered by an opponent. If you are to throw, then throw immediately when you see your team mate open. The best type of throw is the baseball throw. It is quicker in flight than the sling or straight-arm throw. Moreover, if you can, throw the ball to your team mate's feet—it is easier for him to trap.

If you do not see an open team mate near either side line, then stop with the ball—remember you are only allowed four steps with the ball. You are now going to punt the ball. If there is no opponent near you, you can roll the ball to a yard or so from the edge of the penalty area. Pick the ball up when you are standing rather than walking, to avoid taking steps. Either hold the ball in both hands out in front of you or, if you can, hold it in your left hand if you are right-footed. If you are left-footed, hold the ball in your right hand (see illustrations). As you drop the ball (merely take your hand away rather than throw the ball up), step forward onto the non-kicking foot and follow through with your kicking foot onto the ball. Keep your balance and lean forward with your head over the ball.

Good punting and throwing are important aspects of the goalkeeper's game for he is the first offensive player. Moreover, if a goalie throws and punts well, it adds to his team's confidence. No other player affects his team's performance as much as goalkeeper. If the goalie plays with confidence, his team mates will play with confidence. If he panics, his team mates will not play to their best ability.

Besides looking confident, it is easy to inspire your team mates by *sounding* confident. Call "Goalie" for

72–74. PUNTING THE BALL.

each ball you go out to save; shout it so that your fullbacks will hear and not move to play the ball. Whenever the ball is in your penalty area—that is in your territory, and you are the director of the defense—tell your fullbacks what to do. Tell them which opponent to cover. You have the best view of the situation, and you know which opponent is the most dangerous position. You are the last line of defense, so you have to cover for a fullback's error. Similarly, tell one of your fullbacks to cover for you on the goal line if you go out for a ball. The goalkeeper must be his own man in confidence and in directing others, but he must be an integral part of his team's defense. The more you direct play when the ball is in your half of the field, the better your team mates will understand you and have confidence in you as their goalkeeper.

Tips:

1. Move behind the line of the ball before catching it.
2. Watch the ball right into your hands.
3. Recover immediately if you make an error.
4. Know where your goalposts and goal line are.
5. Gather the ball into the chest after catching it.
6. Use two hands to punch the ball.
7. Use the palm of your hands to tip the ball over the crossbar.
8. Always dive on your side.
9. Never hesitate if you decide to go for the ball.
10. Be a master of angles and be in the right place at the right time.
11. Direct your defense; the penalty area is your territory.

13

SPECIAL DEFENSIVE SITUATIONS

Whenever your team has to defend against a corner kick, a direct or indirect free kick, a penalty kick, a throw-in, or even when your team has a goal kick, there are certain reactions the whole team should make so that no scoring opportunity is given away. In school soccer three out of five goals are scored as the result of defensive errors. If your team can eliminate these errors, then you will have a good share of winning games.

The penalty kick: The most threatening of these situations is the penalty kick. The offensive situation was discussed in Chapter 9. Defensively, it is almost entirely the goalkeeper's effort. He must remain with both feet stationary on the goal line until the ball is kicked. A save on a penalty kick is largely an instinctive reaction—even a sixth sense. Actually, a shrewd goalie will: 1) Know if the kicker is right- or left-footed. 2) Watch the kicker at the moment prior to his run toward the ball. At sometime all penalty kickers have to look at which side they are to kick the ball, and this moment is the usual occasion to look. 3) Watch the approach of the kicking foot toward the ball. Most kickers use their instep since it provides the hardest shot. In the approach, one side will appear quite difficult for him to kick the ball toward. Hence, a goalkeeper has at least two methods to determine for which side the kicker is aiming. Also, the goalkeeper should be prepared to push the ball out toward the side line if he cannot hold it so that the kicker has no second shot.

Moreover, in the case of rebounds off the post or the goalie, two fast defensive players should be ready to sprint into the penalty area as soon as the penalty kick is taken. In the case of the goalie saving the ball, the forwards should be alert for a quick counterattack, for most of the opposition will still be wondering why they did not score.

Corners: Beside the penalty kick, the corner presents the most danger for a defense. There are two reasons. First, the corner kick is a direct free kick. That is, the kicker can curve the ball straight into the net. And second, there is no offsides on a corner. This allows offensive players to crowd the penalty area and to wait for the slightest mistake by the defense.

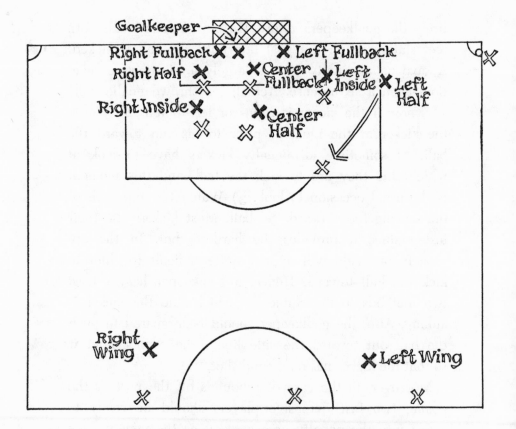

75. DEFENSIVE COVERING ON A CORNER KICK.

The illustration shows a typical defensive setup for a corner kick. Perhaps your team may not even want to leave the two wings upfield for a counterattack. The right and left fullbacks are on the inside of their respective posts with the goalkeeper close to his goal line and the far goalpost. This position prevents the goalie from having to run backward to catch the ball. Two steps backward and he will be able to catch the cross to the far post. If the ball goes to the near post, he can easily run forward to catch it. Furthermore, he should be ready to move out and catch the ball at least as far as the 6-yard line if the ball is crossed in front of the goal. However, watch for the inswinger or outswinger.

All other positions entail covering a man. The defensive man should be between his opponent and the goal. The goalkeeper should call out if there is someone unmarked. In the illustration, the goalkeeper could direct his left half to cover the unmarked opponent in the penalty area. Generally, however, it is a good idea to have someone close to the ball (note that he must be ten yards away from the corner) in case the kicker passes a low cross or miskicks the ball. The left half in his original position could block these balls.

As soon as the ball is cleared out of the penalty area, the goalie should call "Break" and all other defending players should run upfield so that in the event of the ball being chipped back into the penalty area, the opposing forwards will be offside.

Free kicks: Whenever the opposition is awarded a free kick, direct or indirect, the whole team should run back to cover a man apiece. The center forward or an inside should be just ten yards away to block a low ball. Generally, the fullbacks should remain outside of their penalty area in order to have the offside line away from the goalmouth. However, they should be ready to run back into the area to cover a through pass. It is difficult for any player to shoot when he is covered by a defensive player. Remember that your primary duty defensively is to remain between an opposing player and your goal, close enough to him to block a shot and

far enough from him to prevent his dribbling around
you.

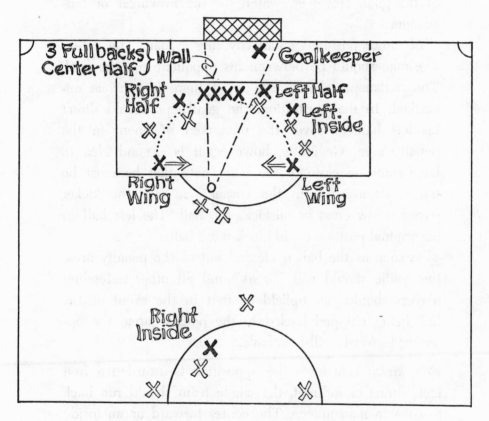

76. DEFENDING A FREE KICK WITH A WALL.

If the opposition is awarded a free kick twenty to
twenty-five yards in front of your goal, the goalkeeper
should direct his defense to form a *wall*. Usually, halfbacks and fullbacks will form the wall. Four players
are sufficient to form a good wall, but the goalkeeper
should decide if he wants more or less players. The
wall is considered most useful when it covers the shot

to the post nearer the ball. In the diagram the wall covers the right goalpost. The goalie stands ready to cover the remaining part of the goal. He should also be ready for a chip over the wall. Since the chip is a lobbed ball, he should have enough time to move across and save it. The remaining team mates should each cover a man, with the goalie directing the coverage. A team may want to leave one player upfield to start a counterattack.

If it is an indirect free kick, often one attacking player will just tap the ball to a team mate standing next to him, who will then shoot. In the illustration you will notice how the right and left wing are ready to move in to block the ball as soon as the ball is first kicked.

As soon as the ball is cleared, or rebounds off the wall, the whole defense should move upfield (except for the goalie). Try to move out of the penalty area quickly. This will prevent opposition forwards staying in front of your goal awaiting a chip pass. If they do, they will be offside. The goalkeeper should shout "Break" as soon as he sees the clearance. All his team mates should remember that he is in charge in the penalty area.

Occasionally, your team might have to defend against a free kick ten yards or less from your goal line. In this case the goalie should call all his team mates back to stand on the line. It is recommended that five players stand on each side of the goal with the goalie covering the gap in the middle. In this situation, if a defender is on the goal line, he does not have to move any farther back even though a free kick is less than ten yards away.

Throw-ins: When the opposition have a throw-in, all of the defending team should run back to cover a man apiece. There should also be a team mate covering the thrower for it is a popular play to pass back to him immediately from the throw. This defensive covering includes the forwards, too, for they should cover each fullback and prevent the throw back to him. An inside or center forward should cover the goalie if the opposition has a throw deep in its half of the field.

Goal kick: Even when your team has a goal kick, the fullbacks should be covering the opposition forwards in case the goal kicker tops the ball, which then rolls out of the penalty area.

Drop ball: If there is a drop ball, it is a direct kick. Hence, the kicker can shoot at goal. This means that even in this situation the defense has to be alert. Moreover, there is no offsides on a drop ball, so cover the opposition forwards.

No team can play without making mistakes, but if everyone covers for each other, scoring opportunities will not be given away.

Tips:

1. Look for the rebound on a penalty kick.
2. Move out of your penalty area after a clearance off a corner kick.
3. Even if you are shorter than your opponent, always challenge for a head ball. You may spoil his timing.

4. Run back to cover a man whenever a free kick or throw-in is awarded to the opposition.
5. Remember the primary duty of a defenseman is to stop the opposition from shooting.
6. Cover for each other, even when your team has a goal kick.

PART III

Further Soccer Ideas

14

ADVANCED
STRATEGY

Even without being able to accomplish the soccer in this chapter, you can be a good soccer player. This chapter is for the knowledgeable and skillful player beyond the junior high level. All these "moves" require much practice to be useful in a game.

Backheeling: The simplest of these is backheeling. It is a pass made with the heel to a team mate directly behind you. Its most common use is to fake forward as if to start dribbling, bringing the foot behind the ball over the ball (for the fake), then simply jabbing at the ball with the heel of the same foot. Step over and *backheel.* Despite its simplicity, it often leads to an interception because the passer does not know who is behind him. You must look around for other possible passes, and then seeing an unmarked team mate behind you, backheel to him as you move forward. The man marking you can either keep marking you—leaving your team mate free to dribble—or the man will leave you to follow the ball. In this case, you should expect the return pass so that you will be free to penetrate the defense.

77. JUMPING TO HEAD THE BALL.

Heading: Although you can usually be more accurate with your heading when you have both feet on the ground, you can win more head balls and score more goals if you are able to jump and head. Here, in the illustration, a player is in position for a header if he jumps. He times his jump, bringing his feet up under him so that he can snap from the waist to head the ball firmly. Make sure you can head the ball on the

forehead—not on the top of the head—as you anticipate your jump. Again, remember, if you are heading
at the goal, jump high enough to be able to head
downward.

78. A DIVING HEADER.

The diving header in the illustration is a way of
being certain in playing the ball. The ball is too low to
head normally and too high to kick easily, so the way
to play it is to lunge or take off at the ball. Aim your
head to meet the ball, keep your hands under your
body, and bring your feet up so that your whole body
goes to meet the ball. Watch the ball onto your forehead. Once again, timing is most important. Generally,
this is used to head at goal or to head away from your
own goal as you intercept the air pass with your head.

Overhead kick: This is almost as spectacular as a goal
from a diving header, but if you miskick the ball with
the overhead kick, you are out of the play. This kick is
used most often by defensemen running toward their

own goal to clear a lob ball that the opposition has kicked over the defenseman's head.

79–80. THE OVERHEAD KICK.

The illustrations show the kicker in action. Notice that the player has jumped up, just before the ball arrives. He leans backward to see the ball, and he is now "in position" to make the kick. Notice that his hands are outstretched under his body.

Penetrating a tight defense: Whenever the opposition mark your forwards so tightly that it is difficult to pass freely and to dribble effectively, the halfbacks can help to create opportunities to penetrate the defense. Here are some ideas. Notice in each case how *space* is *created* for your players to play the ball.

a) If you are a wing halfback seeing all your forwards marked closely, your wing can create space by moving toward the inside (or center forward). Once the defender marking the inside runs with him, pass the ball to where the winger was. The inside can switch positions with the winger by running out to meet the ball.

b) The wing is having trouble dribbling past a good fullback. He receives a pass and moves downfield toward the fullback. However, if the halfback is trailing the play—as he should be—let the wing pass him a ground ball so that he can chip over the fullback's head, first-time, to create space for the wing. As the wing sees the halfback is about to chip, he should spring downfield in anticipation of the pass. The fullback may be a good tackler, but can he recover to avoid being beaten by this play?

c) Often a hustling inside or center forward will work hard to control a ball in the middle of the field in the opposition half. He can wisely create space—dangerous space—by moving laterally with the ball and then quickly passing a ground ball into the opening he has just left. The trailing halfback can run onto the ball for a possible shot or penetration deep into the opposition defense. Again, the fullback marking the inside or center forward has to stay with his man otherwise your forward can penetrate on his own.

In any of these moves, the key is surprise. The goalkeeper is beaten by a surprise diving header. The fullback must be surprised to be beaten. The more plays or moves you know in soccer, the more chance you have to beat your opponent. However, unless you can master a kick, you should not use it in a game. Unless your forwards and halfbacks practice ideas such as these I suggest, they are useless in a game.

Tips:

1. Practice any move before using it in a game.
2. Surprise is the key to penetrating a defense.
3. Try to create space for your team mates.
4. Only try the overhead kick if you can volley clear with either foot.
5. Only try the diving header if you can juggle with your head.

15

PRACTICE AND
GAME PREPARATION

Whether you play soccer on a school team or in a five-a-side make-up game, you will always want to improve. Even with great enthusiasm the player who does not practice his soccer skills will never be a great high-school or a good college player. It is true that Kyle Rote, Jr., did not play soccer until he was seventeen. So you ask yourself why you cannot wait until you are seventeen before taking practice seriously. I can only say that not everyone can practice as hard as Rote does. Moreover, Rote is still learning the game. Yes, there is no substitute for experience. Thus, the sooner you master soccer skills—chip and shoot with either foot, juggle the ball with your head, for example—the higher level of soccer you will be able to reach.

If practice sounds dull, then try some of these drills. By the way, if you do not have your own soccer ball, ask for one for your next birthday!

A: On Your Own:

1. Inside the house try to balance the ball on one foot, or bounce it gently on one thigh. Can you use both thighs then? This bouncing the ball without it touching the ground is called juggling.

2. Outside on your own try to juggle the ball with your head. Top players can even juggle with their shoulder! Then try to juggle with your foot, thigh, or head. Try to break your record each day after you have warmed up.

3. Outside against a stone wall practice accurate passing. Kick the ball ten times against the wall, without trapping, with the inside of the right foot. Now try the left. Switch to using the outside of either foot. Notice the spin on the ball. When you make long passes or shots with the outside of the foot, anticipate this curve.

4. Against a stone wall try the low instep kick. Alternate flicking the ball up in the air and kicking a half volley against the wall.

5. See how many times you can head the ball against the wall without it touching the ground.

B. For Two People:

1. See how many first-time kicks can go back and forward between you.

2. Time how long the two of you can keep the ball off

the ground by passing in the air to each other. Head it or kick it.

3. One person times while the other shuffles the ball between his feet. This is continuous "passing" from one foot to the other. See how many passes can be done in thirty seconds. Fifty is okay, a hundred is excellent.

4. Throw-in to each other. Trap the throw-in, then you throw-in. See how far apart you can move and still be able to throw-in to each other.

5. Play one-on-one with very small goals, such as up-side-down buckets or cones. Winner is the first to score ten goals. Practice your fakes and your tackles in this game.

6. If you can find somewhere wide enough, chip to each other over some obstacle, such as a bush or *small* tree.

7. Punt or drop kick to each other, twenty to thirty yards apart.

8. Take penalty shots at each other. Even if you are not a goalkeeper, you will learn what it is like to be one. Moreover, some tie games now are decided by penalty kicks at the end of regulation time. Every team needs penalty kickers.

C. Team Drills:

1. Five, 6, or 7 a side across half a soccer field using a bench as the goal. No goalies! This can be played as a ground game only if the ball is kicked above waist high; the kicker is penalized by a free kick. Note that two of these games can be played on one field.

2. With players along the goal line and along the half-

way line, chip to each other, calling out the name of the team mate you are passing to. Switch this to volley kicking or half-volley kicking. After trapping a high ball, flick it up in the air with your foot in order to set yourself up for a volley pass.

3. To practice tactics, set up an offensive team and a defensive team. Play on one team for one half. This allows a player to concentrate on defense for a while then switch the teams around so that the former defensive player is now playing in the offensive half of the field. Play ten to fifteen minutes each day. Remember to take throw-ins, corners, and goal kicks for the practice.

4. Split up the team by position.

   a) Have the *wings* dribble down their side line from near the halfway line and center the ball to an *inside* or *center forward* who has been running parallel to the wing. The inside heads or shoots at goal first-time or two-touch. Rotate the *goalkeeper* after every six shots.

   b) At the other end of the field, set the *fullbacks* (including the defensive center half) in front of goal for heading and volley clearing (no goalkeeper). The *halfbacks* chip from the side and from the center of the field to the middle of the penalty area. The fullback who plays the ball must be sure to call for the ball. Pressure can be added by the halfbacks taking long shots at goal which the defenders must try to block or head off the goal line.

   c) Now combine these two drills in one half field.

With a *goalkeeper* and one *fullback,* let the *wing* dribble down his side line with a *center forward* or *inside* square and an attacking *halfback* trailing the play. The three offensive players try to score a goal without being offside. Have the next three attackers ready as soon as the other three finish the play.

5. Again using half field, have three or four *halfbacks* or *forwards* move the ball toward goal with only two *fullbacks* and a *goalkeeper.* It is a good practice in finding the "open" player. Again the offside rule is used. Use both half fields with more than twenty players. Both offense and defense take turns.

6a) A good shooting drill is to use eight balls, placing two at each corner of the penalty box with a player beside them. The shooter stands inside the penalty *arc* and returns to the arc after each shot. The players at the corner of the penalty area feed either ground or chip passes to the penalty spot for the shooter to run onto and shoot either first-time or quickly two-touch He runs quickly back to the arc. As soon as he enters the arc the next ball is passed for him. He is continuously running to shoot or back to the arc so that he has to shoot under pressure and concentrate on timing for all eight balls. The goalkeeper also has a concentrated workout.

b) While the *forwards* and *halfbacks* run through this drill, the *fullbacks* can practice heading and trapping from a long ball. With the goalkeeper punting from his penalty area, the fullbacks, along the halfway line take turns first to trap the punt, then to head the ball. This drill removes all fear from heading for fullbacks! The ball is chipped back to the goalkeeper.

7. If your team has two or more goalies they can drill themselves.

a) Warm up by throwing to each other catching each ball while jumping. Follow this with ten sit-ups with a ball in your hands.

b) One goalkeeper lies on his stomach, with his hands out in front of his face. The other kicks shots at him from about six or seven yards away. Start with soft shots and work up to harder shots —but all shots must be within reach of the goalkeeper. If the shot comes too hard to catch, punch it with both hands. After thirty shots, switch until each goalkeeper has had a turn.

c) The goalkeeper stands on the goal line facing the net. Another throws "shots" at the goal from the edge of the 6-yard box, calling "Go!" as he releases the ball. On "Go!" the goalkeeper turns and has to quickly react to save the ball from entering the goal. Each goalkeeper should try twenty of these "shots."

d) Line ten to fifteen balls up twelve yards away from the goal line, in front of the goal. The goalkeeper has to save each shot from a player who shoots in his own time. The shooter does not wait for the goalkeeper to recover from the last shot, but again forces the goalkeeper to react quickly if he is to try to save each shot.

e) Remember to practice saving penalty shots. Face
ten in a row and then switch.

8. The whole team should practice the special situations
—as corner goal kicks, free kicks near goal, kickoffs,
and even throw-ins. Each player must understand his
position and know where his team mates are in each of
these situations.

D. Game Preparation:

Warm-up drills before a game are essential. The team
should know which drills to do so that each player can
begin to concentrate. A suggested warm up of fifteen
minutes is: Jog around half the field dribbling and
short passing a ball. Short passes in two's or three's,
then throw-in and head or trap. This takes five minutes.

Do some muscle stretching, especially of the legs.
Each player should do a little foot juggling as a ball
becomes available. Spread across your end of the field
to do some chips and long ground passes.

In the last five minutes, *fullbacks* kick stationary balls,
as for a goal kick or free kick; wings can try some corner
kicks, while the other *forwards* and *halfbacks* can shoot
at goal off the corner kicks or off a square pass. No
shooting any stopped balls!

Whenever the captains go to flip the coin with the
referee, the team should stop warming up and gather
around the coach for any last-minute advice. This
might include a warning about the other team's best
players and the weaknesses of their goalkeeper. Listen
to the coach. For example, if he says their goalkeeper

is weak on high balls, a player should think of chipping instead of the long shot.

81. THE BALL SLIDES OR SKIPS IN WET WEATHER.

E. Wet Weather:

Whenever it is raining or the ground is wet, expect the ball to skip or slide along the ground rather than bounce. If it is also muddy, the ball might not even move after landing in a thick patch of mud. Expect the weather conditions to change the style of soccer. Be certain of your clearances on defense in the wet; watch your balance for tackling and your timing for shooting.

What I have said in this chapter are suggestions about practicing. Any coach will have many other drills and ideas. However, your coach is trying to have the whole team understand the same ideas. He may keep the style of soccer simple and, for example, tell you *not* to hold an offside line. Listen to him. He wants *you* to play better soccer and enjoy the game more, so do not fight him.

Beside your coach, your captain is your team's voice. He can ask the referee a question—no one else. Help him to do his job by playing your best for he should be the team's best example of enthusiasm for soccer's sake. Remember it is only a game, and if you lose, what did you learn?

Tips:

1. Practice as much as you can.
2. Practice on your own as well as with the team, since you know your weaknesses in skills.
3. Warm up before a game in silence to concentrate on timing the ball and building up determination.
4. Anticipate mistakes in wet weather.
5. Listen to your coach; help your captain.

The Rules

The rules, or laws, for soccer at school age are based upon the N.C.A.A. rules for colleges. There may be slight changes from time to time, but the fundamental rules of the game will not change. To know the rules is to be able to use them to your advantage. Did you know that there can be no offside from a corner kick, a goal kick, a throw-in, or a drop ball? Here are some important rules worth knowing.

1. The ball must go forward on a kickoff. A goal cannot be scored directly from a kickoff.

2. The ball is still in play when it is *on* the side line or end line. The ball must be *completely* over the boundary lines to be out of play.

3. The ball is still in play when it rebounds onto the field off the goalpost, the crossbar, the corner flag, or even the referee.

4. A player making a throw-in must:
   a) Face the field with both feet off the field of play.
   b) With both hands on the ball, bring it from behind and over the head to release the ball in one even motion. (This means don't spin the ball!)
   c) Keep both feet touching the ground during the

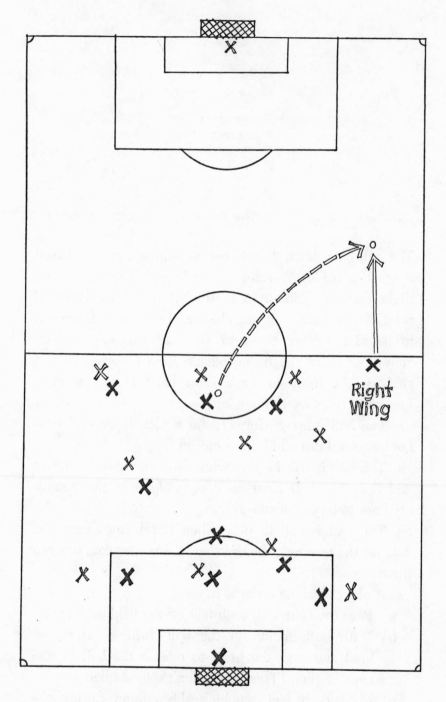

82. NO OFFSIDE IN YOUR OWN HALF.

release. (Drag the back foot if you use the run-up approach.

5. An *indirect* free kick is awarded for offside, delaying the game unnecessarily, ungentlemanly conduct (such as obscene language), arguing with the referee, when the goalkeeper takes more than four steps, obstruction, and dangerous play. (Generally this last point means high kicking or playing the ball when you are on the ground and beside an opponent.)

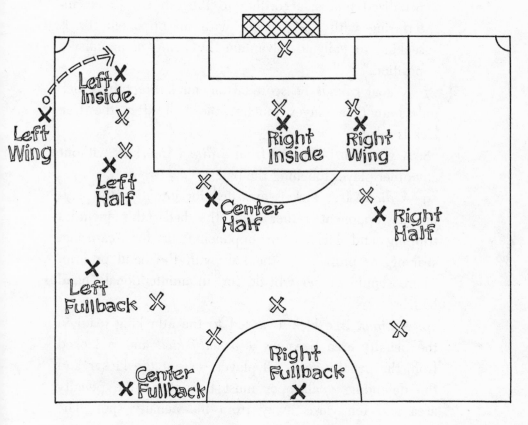

83. NO OFFSIDE FROM A THROW-IN.

6. A player is *offside* if he is nearer the opponent's goal line than the ball *at the moment the ball is last played*, unless:

a) He is in his own half of the field.

b) Two of his opponents are nearer to their goal line than he is.

c) The ball was last touched by an opponent.

d) He received the ball directly from a corner kick, throw-in, drop ball or an opposition goal kick.

However, a player in an offside position shall not be penalized unless, according to the referee, "he is interfering with the play or with an opponent, or is seeking to gain an advantage by being in an offside position."

7. A goal *cannot* be scored from an *indirect* free kick unless another player touches the ball after the free kick is taken.

8. A goal can be scored from a *direct* free kick without any other player touching the ball.

9. A *direct* free kick is awarded for intentionally playing an opponent rather than the ball (this includes tripping and kicking an opponent) or for "carrying, striking, or propelling" the ball with the hand or arm. There should be no whistle for an unintentional "hand ball."

10. A *direct* free kick awarded to the attacking team in the penalty area becomes a *penalty kick* and is kicked from the penalty spot. All players except the kicker and the defending goalkeeper must be outside the penalty area and ten yards away from the penalty spot. The

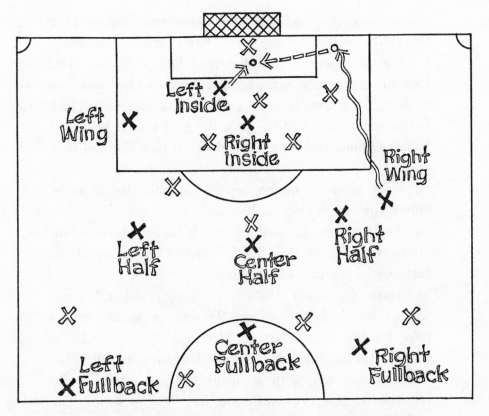

84. NO OFFSIDE WHEN BEHIND THE LINE OF THE BALL.

goalkeeper must have both feet on the goal line until the ball is kicked. The kicker must kick the ball forward and can only kick it once. The ball is in play for all players as soon as the penalty kick is kicked.

11. A *goal kick* is an *indirect* free kick taken from inside the 6-yard box. The ball must be kicked outside the penalty area before another player can play it.

12. A *corner kick* is a *direct* free kick taken from within one yard of the corner flag.

13. On any free kick the opposition must be at least ten yards away from the ball. (Note further restrictions for the penalty kick and the goal kick.) On any free kick there are two whistles; one to stop play and one to restart. (If you score a goal from a direct free kick before the second whistle goes, the goal should be called back!) On any free kick the kicker can play the ball only once.

14. It is legal to nudge or shield with the shoulder only if you are playing the ball too.

15. A player can be sent off the field for obscene language, fighting, or persistently playing an opponent. In this case he is out of the game.

Always remember that even though the rules are written in black and white, the referee interprets the rules for himself. If he sees that a player, after being fouled, still has the ball, he should signal and call "Play on." Perhaps, too, with a "hand ball," the referee did not see it. So play until you hear the whistle. Play with enthusiasm and determination, but play the ball not the opponent for you cannot score goals by kicking a player!

Tips:

1. The rules should be known so that you will be a better soccer player.
2. The referee is an interpreter of the rules. Do not argue with him.
3. Your whole team is often characterized by one bad sportsman.
4. Be a team to be feared because of your hustle not because of your dirty play.

Questions on the Rules

1. On a penalty kick, the ball hits the crossbar and rebounds to the kicker without the goalkeeper ever touching the ball. The kicker kicks the rebounding ball into the goal. Is it a score?

2. On a penalty kick, the kicker rolls the ball a yard forward with the sole of his foot, then a team mate runs into the penalty area and kicks the ball into the goal. Is it a score?

3. The fullback kicks a goal kick, but the ball does not go out of the penalty area. The opposing center forward runs in and kicks the ball into the goal. Is it a score?

4. An attacking player is injured and lying on the edge of the penalty area. He does not move, yet he is in an offside position. A team mate takes a long shot and scores. The goalkeeper protests that the injured player was offside. Is it a score?

5. A player shoots so that the ball is about to enter the goal with the goalkeeper beaten. A fullback desperately dives for the ball. He manages to get a hand on it, but the ball still continues into the net. Is it a score or penalty kick?

6. A fullback is waiting to half-volley a bouncing ball. An opposing forward dives in to head the ball when it is still knee high. Fortunately, the fullback does not kick the forward, but should there be a whistle?

7. A player makes a throw-in. A strong wind blows the ball back and the same player heads it to prevent the ball from going out of play. Should there be a whistle?

8. On a kickoff the center forward kicks a short pass along the halfway line to the inside who dribbles forward. Is there anything wrong?

9. A goalkeeper dives desperately at a shot. He wedges the ball against the inside of the post. The goalie slides over the line into the goal leaving the ball against the post. A fullback comes in quickly to clear the ball. Was it a goal?

10. A defender slips to the ground inside his own penalty area. An opposing forward dribbles past the fallen man who desperately swings with his leg at the ball and kicks the ball out of the area. The forward meanwhile has tripped over the defender's legs. What is the call?

11. On a throw-in a forward runs down to the opposition's end line to await the throw. He receives the throw and crosses the ball. The cross is blocked by a defender, but the ball rebounds to the same forward who is still in an offside position. He then dribbles in to score. Should there be an offside call?

12. A goalkeeper standing in his own penalty area reaches

out and picks up a ball outside the area. Should there be a whistle?

13. An angry goalkeeper, standing with the ball inside his penalty area, throws the ball intentionally at an opponent outside the area. What is the call?

14. A player kicks the ball forward on a kickoff but, seeing that the ball did not reach his team mate, kicks it a second time. Should it be a rekick?

15. The defending team has a free kick in its own penalty area. The kicker passes the ball back to his goalkeeper who punts the ball upfield. Should there be a whistle?

16. The referee is hit by a kicked ball. Should he blow the whistle for a drop ball?

17. A goalkeeper saves a shot and then rolls the ball toward the edge of the penalty area. He does not see an opposing forward approach and steal the ball by nudging the goalie with his shoulder. It is a legal shoulder charge, but can he do so against a goalie?

18. Another goalkeeper substitutes for a team mate after the opposition have just scored their fifth goal. The goalkeeper has reported to the timer's table, then goes in before the kickoff to restart. The first time the new goalie handles the ball, the referee blows his whistle. Why?

19. A fullback and a forward jump up to head the ball, both players trying to go for the ball. They head each other and both collapse injured in front of goal with the ball entangled in their legs. The ref-

eree blows the whistle for the injury. How and where does he restart the game?

20. A player disagrees with a referee and voices his opinion using abusive language. What should the referee do?

Answers:

1. No. Indirect free kick for the defensive team.

2. Yes, provided the team mate was outside the penalty area and was there when the first kick was made.

3. No. The ball is not in play until it goes outside of the penalty area. Rekick.

4. Yes. The offside player was not "interfering with play" or "seeking to gain an advantage by being in an offside position."

5. It is a goal, unless the referee blew his whistle for a penalty kick before the ball entered the goal, in which case the penalty kick must be taken.

6. Yes. It is dangerous play on the part of the player who headed the ball. An indirect free kick for the defensive team.

7. Yes. The penalty for playing the ball twice on a throw-in is an indirect free kick for the opposition.

8. Yes. The ball must be rekicked since it did not go forward on the kickoff.

9. No. If the ball is against the post, it is clearly still on the line. Regardless of the goalie's position, the ball did not fully cross the goal line.

10. Dangerous play could be called against the fullback, even though he kicked the ball. An indirect free kick would then result for the attacking team.

11. No. There is no offside on a throw-in; one cannot be offside if the opposition last played the ball.

12. Yes. Direct free kick from where he handled the ball, which was outside of the penalty area.

13. Penalty kick. The infraction of throwing the ball at an opponent took place inside the penalty area.

14. No. It is an indirect free kick for the opposition.

15. Yes. The ball must be kicked outside the penalty area on any free kick before being passed back to the goalkeeper.

16. No. "Play on" is the correct call.

17. Yes. He can then proceed to score if he can. The goalie did not have possession of the ball when the forward challenged him.

18. The new goalkeeper did not report to the referee. An indirect free kick from where the new goalie first touched the ball with his hands.

19. Play is restarted with a drop ball at the nearest point outside the penalty area to where the collision occurred.

20. He should throw that player out of the game.

Glossary of Soccer Terms

BACKHEEL
To pass behind, or backward, kicking the ball with the heel. See Chapter 14.

BEAT
To dribble around a player or control the ball nearer the opposition goal than the player covering you.

BREAK
To run forward toward the opposition goal with the ball or in anticipation of a pass. Also to run out of one's own penalty area in order to start an offensive movement.

CENTER
To pass the ball from the side to the middle of the field. See Chapter 3.

CHIP
To kick the ball so that it rises over head height and then drops near a team mate. It can be used to pass from twenty to fifty yards away. See Chapter 2.

CLEAR
On defense, to kick the ball long and high toward the halfway line, and usually to the outside.

COVER
On defense, to be in a position to try to stop an opposition player from playing the ball or to stop him from shooting. It is usually best to be positioned

between him and one's own goal. See Chapter 10.

CREATING SPACE
On offense, to make an area free of defenders, for the forwards to use. See Chapter 14.

CROSS
To pass the ball in the air from the side to the middle of the field, or to the other side. Usually a chip. See Chapter 3.

DOG-LEG
On defense, to have the fullback on the opposite side from the ball, nearer his own goal than his team mates, so he can cover for them if they are beaten. See Chapter 10.

DRIBBLE
To run with the ball at one's feet keeping control of it as you run. See Chapter 6.

FEINT
To fake with a movement of the body or to fake a kick. See Chapter 6.

FIRST-TIME
To play the ball without trapping it.

GIVE-AND-GO
To make a short pass to a team mate who returns the ball first-time to you as a lead pass. See Chapter 3.

HALF-VOLLEY
To kick the ball at the moment it bounces. See Chapter 2.

INSIDE
The central part of the field, away from the side line. Also, the forward who plays in the central part of the field.

INSIDE OF THE FOOT	The part of the foot that faces the other foot when standing.
INSTEP	The part of the foot under the laces of the soccer shoe. See Chapter 2.
INSWINGER	A centering pass that curves toward the goal, especially on corner kicks.
JOCKEY	To be able to keep an opposition forward where the defender wants him, and to restrict his dribbling.
LEAD	To pass ahead of a team mate so that he can run onto the ball.
LINK	A mid-field player who links the full-backs and the forwards on offense and assists the fullbacks on defense.
LOB	A high but not powerful kick.
LOFTED INSTEP KICK	A long high kick made with the inside of the instep.
MARK	Same as to cover or to guard a player.
MOVE OFF THE BALL	To move away from the player with the ball, to create running space for him.
OFFSIDE	See the rules in Appendix I.
OUTSIDE	Any part of the field near the side line. Also, the wing.
OUTSWINGER	The centering pass that curves away from the goal. This happens when the

right wing chips a center with his right foot, especially on corner kicks.

SQUARE — Lateral or sideways of a player. Often a lateral ground pass of ten to fifteen yards. See Chapter 3.

STRIKER — An attacking player who is positioned to be able to threaten and "strike" at the opposition goal. He is an inside or center forward.

SWEEPER — The center fullback who plays behind his other fullbacks as an extra or safety defender. He can cover for any other fullback who is beaten.

TACKLE — To take the ball away from a player using your feet. It must be without touching him before playing the ball. See Chapter 11.

THROUGH BALL OR PASS — An attacking or penetrating pass that goes behind the line of fullbacks. See Chapter 3.

TRAIL — To support a team mate from behind, running ten to fifteen yards behind him or the play.

TRAP — To stop the ball as it comes toward you and to control it immediately; that is, to keep it within playing distance. See Chapter 5.

TWO-TOUCH

To touch the ball twice; once to trap or control the ball, then to pass or shoot immediately.

VOLLEY

To kick the ball that is still in the air without trapping it. See Chapter 2.

WING

The forward or attacking player who is positioned close to the side line. He is usually very fast.

WING HALF

The right or left halfback. He trails the wing on offense and covers on defense—usually an opposition inside forward.

Brian Lindsay Denyer was born in England and attended school in Scotland. Like millions of Scottish schoolboys, he was able not only to play soccer all the year round but also to watch the local professionals each Saturday in a club game. Occasionally, he had the opportunity of seeing Scotland play in an international game.

Mr. Denyer came to the United States to attend Amherst College in Massachusetts, where he received his B.A. in 1970. After playing college soccer, he began teaching and coaching the game at the King School in Stamford, Connecticut. Beside being the school's head soccer coach, he is a member of the Southern Connecticut Soccer Officials Association and still plays in the Connecticut League. He has also visited several soccer camps during the summer as an instructor.

John Lane, artist and illustrator, is chief editorial cartoonist of Newspaper Enterprise Association. His cartoons are distributed to NEA's more than 750 daily newspaper subscribers in North America. He joined NEA as a staff artist in 1956 and has been the firm's creative art director for the past six years. Since that time he has covered two presidential elections, including the national conventions, the races at Daytona, and several major trials, providing on-the-spot sketches of personalities and events.